"Gunther Karger has had an amazing life and an inspirational story to tell. It is a story of courage, perseverance, hard work and intelligence, and an extraordinary partnership with his wife, Shirley. This book is a reminder to all of us that the American Dream is indeed possible."

Mary L. Schapiro
Former Chairman
U.S. Securities and Exchange Commission

"As a highly respected author, market analyst, investor and "serial" philanthropist, Gunther Karger has distinguished himself as a notable commentator on the affairs of the day. Drawing on his extensive experience he has written several interesting and well documented books. Arriving in this country as a young "Holocaust Survivor," he rose to an aviation executive and an accomplished author, Gunther now focuses on his interest in commentating as a Futurist and the impact on him personally and the potential solutions to global issues. I have been privileged to call Gunther and his wife, Shirley, friends and hold them in a special place in my personal and business life."

S. Albert Hanser
Founder, CEO & Chairman
The Sanibel Captiva Trust Company, Florida
Former Board Member – Mayo Clinic

"Gunther Karger is an accomplished author, a student of history and an astute observer of the human condition – and a very smart and insightful guy. He possesses a remarkable ability to translate a deep knowledge of past events to provide a historical perspective to contemporary issues that effect us all. His new book provides us a clear and concise foundation for the tough decisions, we as a society, need to deal with in addressing the complex economic and geopolitical issues facing us today."

Brian E. Keeley
President & CEO
Baptist Health South Florida
Coral Gables, Florida

"Gunther Karger's road traveled is an amazing story told with little emotion for the bad and challenging times and great joy for the good times. Love does not always flow along blood lines and Gunther memorialized some of the kind folks who were along his path from Nazi Germany and the Holocaust to freedom and great personal success in the United States. The U.S. Air Force was his spring board.He was a part of the Silicon Valley of the East in northern New Jersey and then into the Space Program. Gunther's vision as a futurist is darker than mine but nonetheless his vision is important to explore given the path that he has traveled with his loving wife Shirley."

Bob Jensen
Commander US Navy, Ret
Historian and author, Homestead, Florida

" I met Gunther on his visit to his German hometown and listened to his incredible history, the unimaginable intellectual rise which was his, his integration in the space rocket teams of Cape Canaveral working with former German rocket scientist Wernher von Braun despite everything that he had lived. And, if I had already much admiration for Gunther and Shirley(because one does not go without the other), this book which testifies to this amazing life at the same time so painful and so rich, definitely makes me realize that I was incredibly lucky to cross what the Yiddish world calls a "Mensch". In the so complex and hard world that we all created, it is necessary to listen and to hear the voice of men like Gunther."

Evelyne Dreyfus
Journalist and film producer
Paris, France

Also by Gunther Karger

Thieves on Wall Street
Wall Street and Government Fraud
Wisdom and Humor in Business
Your Plan to Success
International Space Log
The Discovery Letter
Discovery Lectures aboard Cruises

Gunther Karger

My Life
Rising from the ashes of the Holocaust
and
Global Society Rising

Cover and book design by Gunther and Shirley Karger

Published in the United States by
Gunther Karger
Website: **www.guntherkarger.com**

ISBN: 13: 978-1502467911

For inquiries, contact Gunther Karger
2275 SE 4th Ct.
Homestead, Florida, USA 33033
e-mail: Gunther@ieee.org

Courage

As you read this book, remember my parents who were Herbert and Ida Karger. A couple aged only 45 years old, suddenly realizing they and their son could face near certain death if not a horrific existence in captivity and persecution. They had two choices. To keep their family together and await disaster that lay for near certain ahead. Or send their only son, just six years old away to distant land and strangers they did not know.

They chose new life for their son. They put him on a train with him not knowing why or what was happening. He was placed into the void of a new world they did not know except that he had a better chance for life instead of near certain death. They knew their son was the last of the family that had lived in their home for 250 years. Through him, the Karger family could continue or tragically end.

Their son, "awoke" from a deep slumber in a strange land, sitting on a black suitcase with an address tag around his neck. He saw no familiar face. Only strangers speaking a strange language. He didn't know who he was or where he came from. Only the tag round his neck told this. A stranger speaking an unfamiliar language then put him on a train but he knew not its destination. It left the station for a new life he knew none of.

Gunther's parents soon were taken from their ancestral home along with his grandparents. To the mountains of southern France near Spain. To a camp not fit for humans where his grandparents did not survive hunger and illness. Two year later, in 1942, his parents then only 47, still together having survived thus far, were put on a cattle train bound for a human slaughterhouse hundreds of miles away and murdered in a gas chamber on arrival

I am their son. The six year old boy sent away alone in the night. When I learned who I was and who my parents were, I made this promise to them.

"To do my best carrying forward their memory and make my life count for something. They lived with courage, they practiced courage, they died because of their courage.

As you read this book, I hope you will agree that I did my best to keep that promise. I also hope that you will, even if it's just for a moment, know and remember that they existed and what they did to make sure their only son would survive one of the most horrendous tragedy of all times, the Holocaust.

I am **Günter Karger,** Born in Schmieheim, Germany, March 16, 1933 to parents Herbert and Ida Karger. Today is 2014, 81 years later.

This was one of several pictures I found in an envelope in the black suitcase telling me who I was and where I came from. The picture is of my parents, Herbert and Ida Karger and myself Günter. It was taken in 1939 just before I was sent to Sweden to escape the Holocaust.

Gunther & Shirley Karger

Shirley Rosenzweig Karger born 1934, in NewOrleans,
La. We met in 1951 at Keesler AFB, Biloxi, Miss.
Married December 5, 1954 - Partners for life

"When money speaks, truth keeps silent"

Why did I write this book?

Shirley & I(it's been 'Shirley & Gunther" for the 60 years since we married) have for several years considered what should be our legacy. The no brainer thing is to leave it to the kids and they'll carry on our work carrying our family to the future or have enough money to leave a financial legacy to continue on our work.

My original hope was to have our two sons join us and carry on. But we have known for many years that was not to be. Until the recent financial meltdown, we had hopes of creating a scholarship and a teaching chair at a university (LSU). We were on our way with this path but the financial crisis of 2008 destroyed this option.

Then came my 81st birthday ringing the bell!. It's now or never. If we don't right now create some legacy for the rich life we have had and how we contributed to society, all that would be soon lost. The awards on my wall would be taken down and thrashed with the rest at Goodwill. There would be no grand children to even remember our existence. So, I'll instead list a few significant awards in an appendix to this book. You'll probably never again hear of having an "appendix" instead of grandchildren as part of a family legacy.

I had considered writing a third major book telling how our world would dramatically change over the next 25 years thanks to the deteriorating political structure of the United States. But who would believe what I foretell in advance of a quarter of a century without first having known my history of credentials?

The second bell rang in June , 2014 sitting in the chemo chair at the Miami VA Hospital. No, I am not dying (yet) but have for two years had a nagging skin lymphoma (blood cancer). It won't kill me but does need maintenance so I don't scratch myself to death.

My Life – Global Society Rising

The next bell rang with the song "Time is up! Decide your legacy and make it happen". I listened and that night told Shirley what the bell tolled.

Many people have told me that I should write a book on my life. I actually helped write the book "Children who survived the final solution" wherein one chapter titled "Child of the Holocaust" tells of my escape from the Holocaust. But that's no "legacy" nor would my latest two books "**Thieves on Wall Street**" and "**Wall Street and Government Fraud**" make that grade.

The final bell gave me the answer. Independence Day (July 4th) is just round the corner and for the second consecutive year I am invited to play (on my famous harmonica) "**God Bless America**" before at least 15,000 people at the Homestead Championship NASCAR Speedway Fireworks extravaganza sponsored by the city of Homestead, Florida (near Miami).

That same day at 11:00 am, I was scheduled to play just before the F-16 flyover at the Palmetto Bay Independence Day Celebration. This followed me being awarded "The Distinguished Citizens Award and Medal" by the United States Marine Corps League for service in Korean war with special mention of my work in the Cold War when I received a national award for possibly saving the country from a nuclear attack(in a role remindful of the "Jack Ryan" CIA thrillers).

Then a year ago I received a special Certificate of Appreciation from none other than the Chairman of the United States Securities and Exchange Commission who also made me an honorary Special Federal Agent recognizing me personally and singularly helping the SEC get through the worst financial crisis since the Great Depression.

This for a war orphan who arrived to these shores at age 13 in 1946 with nothing and alone suggests that my life does have some lasting meaning.

The bell tolled the title of the book which will become my legacy "**My Life – Rising from the ashes of the Holocaust and Global Society Rising**". The legacy part of this will impart the experience and wisdom many people told me I exhibited over the years despite huge odds.

I also tell the world and especially politicians what they must do to avoid losing their country. In this book, I describe the new world that's coming unless leaders change the way they lead. As I have in my prior books and reports , I also tell what can and must be done to resolve the problems I present.

I believe strongly that no person should ever criticize anything unless also is presented a way to resolve the problem or at least make things better. Thus, maybe in future years I might be remembered as a *Gunther the Prophet.*

The "gift" of observing a constantly evolving complex world and sharing my views and predictions of what may yet to come came to me by the life I was given by my parents, all of you who came into my life thereafter and the experience all that offered.

This book is my "legacy". I wrote it in my hope that sharing the life I was given will in a small way help shape a better future world.

I urge you to read the "Table of content" because it gives an overview of this book

Gunther Karger, 2014, Age 81

"Life belongs to the living, and he who lives must be prepared for change"
Johann Wolfgang von Goethe

Dedication

First, I dedicate this, my final book, to Shirley, my wife of 60 years, who accepted a stranger with no money and whose entire family perished in the Holocaust. By standing with me all these years, she made all this possible despite many very difficult times. Without Shirley, this book could not be written nor would you ever have even heard of Gunther Karger.

SECOND, I thank my parents, Herbert and Ida Karger, for having the courage and wisdom to send me, their only child, away to the safety in another country knowing that If they did not, I would surely be murdered along with them and my grand parents by Hitler's Nazis. I have always honored their memory by doing my best in all that I was able to do and by telling of their existence while I was able so they too would be remembered, at least for a while.

THIRD, I thank all of you who received our newsletters, reports, epistles and whatever you may call my outpourings. Without you, I would not have learned what I did. It's the knowledge I received from all of you throughout these many years that much of what I was able to do was made possible. For all of this, I deeply thank you.

Acknowledgements

There is no doubt this book nor much of anything I have written would ever have seen the "day of light" were it not for Shirley, my wife, friend for life and Editor in Chief of most of what I have written. Be it newsletters, reports or whatever comes out of my keyboard, she reviews, offers comments and catches errors.

I must also acknowledge all those of you who received "The Discovery Letter" over the past 30 years and encouraged me to continue on. I thank you all for that.

How this book is structured

The first part of this book tells my life's story and experience "Rising from the ashes of the Holocaust".

The second part tells of a world transitioning toward a global society ending with how I believe the United States resolves its declining world influence by dramatically changing its own political system. I continue this "transition" beyond the present 2014 through the following twenty years to 2035.

My fervent wish is that somehow this book finds it way to the hallways of todays leaders, especially those in Washington to remind them of the extreme importance to well learn and respect the lessons of history. It is my opinion that this country's national leadership lost its way since 9/11 by either ignoring history, not knowing it due to inadequate education or simply a lack of experience in managing complex systems. There has been entirely too much eloquent speechmaking instead of courageous deeds.

As it was in the beginning when America was created, a general, General George Washington, took charge to create a great country, soon, another general will take charge to rescue America.

I suggest you actually read through the Table of Content because it tells you what this book covers. The chapters are brief addressing specific singular topics.

Table of Content

BOOK 1 - MY LIFE

GERMANY

SWEDEN

AMERICA – EARLY YEARS

BUILDING MY LIFE

BOOK 2
GLOBAL SOCIETY RISING   210

My Origin- Nazi Germany

I am from Schmieheim, Germany. It's a small town population of about 1200 nestled in the southwest corner of Germany between France and Switzerland on the west70n slopes of the Black Forest. The main industry is its only brewery with its own restaurant. We lived at 100 Schlossstrasse, almost across the street from the town's 600 year old castle where on its second floor was my kindergarten.

**Schmieheim 1938 & my kindergarten class
(Gunter top row 4th from left)**

Gunther Karger

Downtown Schmieheim early 1900's

Gunther & parents Herbert and Ida Karger 1939

The area in Germany I am from is known as the Baden region which became a haven for many Jews escaping the Spanish Inquisition in the 1400-1500's and the pogroms of Eastern Europe in Poland - Ukraine. The Jewish population rose as high to 50% of some town populations which suggests that at the turn of the 19th Century nearly 500 Jews made Schmieheim their home.

Resulting from escalating Jewish population, by year-end 1939 only 14 Jews remained in Schmieheim. Early winter 1940, just a few months after I was sent to Sweden, all were arrested, deported and killed in concentration camps in southern France and Poland. Of these last Jews, eight were my own family including my very own parents and grandparents. Today, no Jews live in Schmieheim.

Gunther Karger

My Memory of Nazi Germany
1933 - 1939

I lived with my family for six years, born in 1933, the same year Adolph Hitler became Chancellor of Germany. My memory of my first six years of childhood while living with my parents in Germany is very limited. The only memory I have of this time is limited to only four specific recollections.

- My father playing piano
- My grandfather who lived in Berlin taking me to see and hear Hitler speak once downtown Berlin. I clearly remember the mass of steel helmeted soldiers with the red and black Swastika arm bands marching and Hitler's inner circle ministers riding in their huge Mercedes touring car to the front with the shouting of "Sig Heil" and their arms outstretched.
- My uncle Manfred visiting our home in Schmieheim on his motor cycle with my aunt Elsa riding in the side car
- Playing in the street with my friend, Hanna Baumann.

What you read here is the sum total of my direct memory of living in Germany with my family. I remember nothing else. Not even my mother. It's like my memory of the first six years of my life having been erased. Except for these four direct and clear memories. I have been told that my early childhood memory was erased or relegated to unreachable places in my brain caused by a traumatic event.

All else I know of my Germany childhood I learned by what I was told by others about what happened to my family, my home and early childhood.

Psychologists encouraged and offered to reach into my subconscious via hypnosis and other means for me to remember but I ran the other way every time that was offered. They thought it was important for me to remember but I thought it was more important for me to not allow these mind benders to mess with my mind and for me to live with the life I was "dealt" by the world given me to live in. I felt it was more important to focus on "the rest of my life" which always lies ahead than dwell on the details of my past which was irretrievably gone and probably a very dark "place".

This ruled my life allowing me to gain an unusual and focused memory with detailed recall of all that I encountered since my exit from Germany. It's like my direct memory of life in Germany with my family was erased so that the son who survived could live on.

I have always felt that too many people with a troubled past dwell so much on that past that they destroy the future they could have.

It's from this that came the expression I created and so often use in writings, speeches and discussions

"*The hands of time move forward to the right. Whosoever tries to turn that clock back stops him from moving to the future*" – Gunther Karger

The Hannah Baumann Murder

Hannah Baumann was the last Jewish person born in Schmieheim. She was my kindergarten classmate and we played in the streets. Like me, she was an only child and one year younger than me, born in 1934.

Hanna Baumann & Gunter

Kristallnacht was that night on November 9, 1938 when gangs of Nazi ravaged through the streets of German cities throwing rocks breaking the glass on Jewish store fronts plundering them, dragging out store owners with their families beating them up. Some were arrested and taken to the police station.

Although Schmieheim escaped the ravages of Kristallnacht (Night of Broken Glass), the Baumann family fled together, parents taking Hannah with on a train out of town in 1939. But they did not escape. The train was stopped by Nazi soldiers, forced all Jews off the train. Then, they shot them all throwing their bodies along the rail siding and buried them in the ground, including the Baumanns, and my little friend, Hannah.

Although I don't know this directly, I always suspected that my parents took a lesson from this when they found a way to send me away on the last train shipment of Jewish children out of Germany to Sweden. Although it was too late for them to escape, they found this way out for me. I lived but they were all murdered, including my grand parents and other relatives.

How Gunther escaped the Holocaust

The HIAS,(Hebrew International Aid Society) had arranged for 500 children six and younger to be rounded up throughout Germany to be placed on trains bound for a ferry from Hamburg to Malmo in the southern tip of Sweden. HIAS had issued a call to the Pentecostal Church of Sweden to take in as many of these children as possible until they could be returned to their families. I was one of these children, the only one from my hometown.

I have no recollection of this nor even remember my parents putting me on a train nor saying goodbye. Years later, I was told that all this had to be done in secret and quickly. I learned much later that I was never again to see my parents, grandparents and some aunts and uncles. What happened to my family after they sent me away?

How the Nazis murdered my family

There are some who even today question why so many Jews didn't leave before it was too late. That's a very good question. Unlike today when we have TV, internet and all kinds of personal instant communications letting us know firsthand and nearly immediately what's happening as it happens nearly regardless where in the world it's happening, none of that existed then. The Nazi propaganda machine also made sure that whatever was already happening at the emerging concentration camps mostly in Eastern Germany and Poland was tightly kept secret.

I learned not until just a few years ago that my parents tried to leave for South America and asked a relative living in Uruguay to sponsor them but were refused. So my parents were arrested along with the rest of the remaining 14 Jews of Schmieheim early winter of 1940 and transported to a concentration camp in the Pyrenees mountains in France along the Spanish border. This was mostly a slave labor camp where the people were worked or starved to death which happened to my grandparents who already were in their early 80's.

When Camp de Gurs closed early 1942, the inmates able to survive the harsh existence they were forced to endure were placed on cattle trains and shipped like animals to the Auschwitz death camp in Poland. On arrival, they were murdered in the gas chambers after stripping them of their remaining belongings. They both were only in their mid 40's.

While in the French concentration camp, my father was able to send a few brief letters and post cards to me in Sweden. I have all these original letters the last one postmarked May, 1942.

These letters along with all that happened to me as I grew up without family, led me to the obsession of creating something for the world to remember my parents. As it turned out, not having grand children to carry on, it could only become the good deeds I was able to make over the years. This became an obsession to right the wrongs I saw all around me by so many people.

Following our official visit to Schmieheim in 2003, the Schmieheim Church youth group under the leadership of Pastor Matthias Krepling and his wife, Renate, created a memorial stone outside their church commemorating those last 14 Jews of Schmieheim and my family. May the 14 permanent lights around this memorial tell the world that my parents did exist and be remembered even for just a little while longer beyond me, their only survivor. This memorial is shown below.

What Gunther's family left him

The Offenheimers of Schmieheim(my mother's family name was Ida Offenheimer) had lived in Schmieheim since the early 1700's. When we visited Schmieheim during our official visit at the invitation of Burgermeister (Mayor) Willy Mathis, we attended the unveiling of the restored Jewish cemetery where my great grand father was buried in 1752. This is the picture of Shirley & me by that stone.

This cemetery was restored by the local area Historical Society sponsored partly by the local town as part of Germany's effort to restore Jewish history and atone for the unspeakable human atrocities committed by Hitler's regime.

We participated in the unveiling of this restored old cemetery.

My parents lived in my mother's ancestral home with my grand parents, Gustav and Sara Offenheimer on Schlossstrase 100(Castle Street) nearly across the street from the 600 year old castle where I went to kindergarten. When they were arrested and dragged out of their own home, our home became abandoned, plundered and just rotted from the harsh winters, snow and ice.

The German government confiscated the property and eventually sold it to a German family for $500. The new owner rebuilt it from the rubble it had become. During our 2003 visit, we were invited in for coffee and cake in the house once that belonged to my family.

My grandparents Gustav & Sara Offenheimer, the house they built for my parents and the legacy they left.

These are the ashes Gunther came out of and what eventually motivated him to do what he continues to do over his life which as of this writing is 81 years. It is to the memory of this family that this book is dedicated. As you will read on in this book, it is a miracle that not only did I survive this, but also the disasters I faced and survived over the years. There is more than one person who referred me to as "the Second Moses" saved by his family so he could save the world in later years.

My family gave me "Life" and nothing else. I was robbed of my childhood, memory of having love and affection from parents, The Holocaust left me with no worldly possessions. I should be known as "Child of the Holocaust" given "life" by parents who sent me away at age six so I could live as they were brutally murdered when they were only about 45 years of age.

But my parents also gave me opportunity to learn to become strong and survive through many ordeals. The legacy I want to leave in their honor is that the person they brought to the world and saved in at least a small way paved the road toward a better future world.

Gunther Karger, 2014, age 81

Biblical prophetic reference

"Josef was saved to interpret the Pharaoh's dreams of what's yet to come leading to Moses who was saved by his Mother eventually to lead his people to the Promised Land. "

Rebirth at Age 6 in Sweden, 1939

The little boy, age 6 sat on a wooden black suitcase in the midst of a great train station. Tall blond people were milling around speaking a language he didn't understand. Around his neck hung an address tag where the boy was being shipped. The little boy didn't know where he was, didn't know where he came from, how he got there nor knew where he was going. He was all alone in a strange new world. The tag around his neck gave his name "Günter Karger".

I was that little boy. Until that moment, I recall nearly nothing, From that moment, I remember nearly clearly all and slowly gained some knowledge of who I was and why I had come to "such a place". I had been "reborn" into a new life starting not at "birth", but at age six, in a train station, sitting on a black suitcase containing all my worldly possessions arriving to a new life.

In truth, this is the "image" that I was "born" with" and what remains with me all these 75 years later. This "image" has been the psyche of so often having that "alone" feeling of always having to super rely on myself, always doing my best to know "where and what's next for me". It is the thought ingrained into my mind that I am focused on the future and always trying to anticipate what that would be. This image also became the driver of me trying to make the "future" more secure and defined.

It led to my lifelong focus on trying to anticipate the unknown and learning all about it. This obsession with the future and unknown is likely what led me into science, the search for truth which eventually led me to the comic strip "Kapten Frank" who was the Swedish equivalent to Buck Rogers and predecessor to Flash Gordon who pioneered science fiction as the guardians of galactic universe.

There is no doubt that the image stemming from my "rebirth" and somehow ingrained "God given" focus on understanding the "future" is what eventually led me to become a real scientist exploring the unknowns on earth and in space. This likely is what guided me through a lifelong journey along which I met and worked with such historic persons including Dr. Vernher von Braun, the German rocket engineer who developed Hitler's V2 rocket and later America's first manned space craft(after the Russians beat America).

I honestly believe that it's this ingrained image of a lone boy facing the unknown that eventually takes us to the "appendix" of this book listing some of my accomplishments such as named 'Outstanding Young Engineer of the Year" by the world's largest electrical engineering organization(1965), Outstanding Young Man of America, (1967), "Fellow of the British Interplanetary Society" and founding member of the original "Cape Canaveral Missile and Space Pioneers" which delivered America into Space and other scientific frontiers.

It is this unending search for the unknown that led Shirley & me to the 2010 gathering of space pioneers at which I took a picture of Shirley with Astronaut Bob Crippen who was the command pilot of the Manned Orbital Laboratory and the first command pilot of the Space Shuttle.

It was my "rebirth" at age six in Sweden, sitting atop of that black suitcase alone among total strangers in a train station that evolved into the person I eventually became. By all reasonable standards, it is a miracle that I survived such ordeals and challenges I encountered during the 75 years that followed.

Astronaut Bob Crippen and spacecraft launch control center director Andy Anderson with Shirley at The Rocket Pioneer Gathering, Cocoa Beach Hilton, 2010

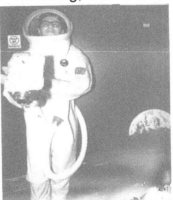

Gunther in a real space suit at the Houston Manned Space Center, 1975

Gunther in Sweden

I was sent to live with the Gustafsson family who were tenant farmers in Stora Skedvi in the Dalarna province of northwest Sweden and arrived by train and bus. This was a small village along the Dalalven river. My new "family" became Karl Gustafsson, his wife Hanna and their 7 year old daughter, Ragnhild. (Ragnhild is a Viking name))

I knew no Swedish and Farbror (uncle) Karl nor anyone in the village knew any German. The pastor of the village church knew a little German and he helped us starting to communicate.

This was my rebirth in a new world with new language, strangers and ways. I was the only black haired person and shortest in the village as all others were tall and blond. None of them had ever even seen a Jewish person before.

I arrived with my one black suitcase which had all my possessions. A few clothes and an envelope with a few pictures of what I later learned were my parents and family in Germany. This envelope had the picture of Hanna Baumann and me which many years later became famous when the new kindergarten in Schmieheim was named and dedicated to her.

The Gustafssons were devout Christians attending the church Sunday mornings, bible meetings in the village's only school Sunday nights. They were strict, demanded respect and that everyone in the house did their given jobs on the farm.

The Gustafsson's lived in a small house as tenant farmers with the larger house belonging to the owner who came in from Stockholm in summers. We had no car or truck to use on the farm which produced potatoes and rye. They had several cows for milk and one of my jobs was to "milk" the cows by hand. The two horses were used for plowing (with a hand plow), transporting hay and the harvest with a wagon.

The house had no toilet and we had to use an outhouse. That was tough during the winters when the average temperature was 40 degrees minus with snows coming late August through April. They didn't have a refrigerator but placed food in the cellar which was always cold enough.

When we took a bath in summer, we went to the river which flowed next to the farm and just took a swim. In the winters, there was a small shack with a wooden barrel sawed in half sitting on top of a grate under which a fire was started to heat the water.

The village had two schools. One was a one room school for the first grade with one teacher, Fru (Mrs.) Anderson. The other was a larger school house with the rest of the grades and the headmaster who lived in a house on the school grounds. There were no such things as school buses so when there was no snow, I was given a bicycle and during winters, everyone got to school on skis.

The village had one store which also had a small movie room. But the Gustafsons didn't allow us (their daughter of me) to see movies or any socials like dances because of their strict religious practices. They were strict Pentecostal Christians.

I lived with the Gustafssons for five years and they treated me like I were part of their family. I learned the need for hard work to earn a day's existence, respect for elders and the importance of obedience to rules which in such harsh environment is a necessity for survival.

Everyone in the village were friends and acted as one family each helping one another in time of need. There was one community steam house used by men Friday nights and women Saturday nights mostly during the winter as the river could be used when there wasn't snow and ice. I learned that one had to cool down quickly before going out into the sub zero freezing night(in winters, it was always "night" because daylight was only for about an hour midday. This was in the artic north just south of the Artic circle. The quick "chill down" was simply to go outside and roll in the snow. The braver men sawed a hole in the river ice and dipped in the ice water.

The farm was on the bank of Sweden's largest river with the water coming off the mountains and forests near Norway and running all the way out to Baltic Sea across which lies Finland. This river as well as the Baltic sea always was frozen solid with ice in winters.

During winters when there can be no farming because of snow and ice, the men go out in the forest and cut down trees for timber. The timber is taken down to the river to float to the downriver mills. During summers, I often went to the river to fish and ride the rolling logs downstream .

Gunther & Ragnhild, Winter 1942, Sweden

Gunther & Ragnhild Gustafsson
If I would have a sister, it would be Ragnhild. We
both are still alive, she at 82, me 81(as of 2014)

Karl Vilhelm Gustafsson on his 80th in 1972

Karl Gustafsson to me was "Farbror Karl" and the head of the family which gave me a home when I had none, a "father" when I no longer had parents and much wisdom. I will be forever grateful to him and his family to have given me a "family" and home when I had lost mine.

Stora Skedvi Kyrkan, One of Europe's oldest churches built around 1200, restored in 1600's. My name is inscribed in the bell tower

**My first grade class.
There was only one classroom
and one teacher, Fru (Mrs.) Anderson**

Gunther and music

The black suitcase with all my possessions from Germany had a harmonica. Soon, it became known in the village that the stranger had musical talent. The church pastor found an old violin in the church basement, gave it to me and arranged music lessons. The violin is a Stradivarius copy made in Germany sometimes in the 1800's.

When I was taken away from my Swedish foster family after 5 years in 1944 at age 11, I was allowed to take with me that violin which today is still with me hanging on the walls of my study.

Over the years, I became known as the Harmonica Man and was invited to play for events. During our "Official visit" to Schmieheim in 2003, the mayor invited me to play the original German Waltz I had composed years before "the Schmieheimer Waltz" for the annual wine festival.

As I write this in June, 2014, I am getting ready to play "God Bless America" at the city's annual 4th of July Independence Day and July 4th fireworks celebration at the Homestead Championship Speedway where 15,000 people are expected and early that day just before the Air Force F-16's fly overhead in military formation

I am also invited as a special guest at the area 'Summer Music Festival" given by the area church community church choir.

Am I Jewish or Christian?

The Gustafssons were devout church going Christians. They considered me part of their family and made me feel I belonged somewhere. I much later learned that there was talk of even adopting me since I really had no family nor anyplace else to go.

This "peace" came abruptly to an end when I was told in 1944, after 5 years with the Gustafssons, that I would be leaving because the organization which arranged the escape from Germany was afraid I would be lost to my Jewish heritage.

So, one day, I was told to pack that black suitcase where once again it all went and I was put on another train to the unknown. Once again, this time as an 11 year old boy, I was sent away into the unknown to strangers. But this time, I also had a second black case holding the violin the church pastor had given me and that violin was to never leave my side. Even today, it hangs on the wall of my office.

The next "stop" for me was a Jewish orphanage in Osby on a lake in southern Sweden. This was to be my "next" home but only for a year. This was the place I would be 'reminded" that I was Jewish.

Look for the chapter in this book giving my thoughts on "Religion" to answer this question. My view is that there are far too many religions and variants of religions and that religion has been used to start wars, kill people and cause far more problems than it's supposed to solve.

Gunther Karger

The Orphanage

The orphanage was operated by a Jewish agency out of Stockholm and was a large house with many bedrooms each holding two bunk beds sleeping four. There were both boys and girls totaling maybe about a dozen with the "house" managed by a head lady, Fru Levy and a housekeeper/cook, Fru Schlesinger.

I remember a simple and unchanging routine . Getting up in the morning, making the bed, a common breakfast and off to school. For Friday dinner was a candle lighting with Jewish readings. While 'Jesus" was a normal thing at Gustafsson's farm and I probably had attended several revival meetings where I may even had been "saved", any mention of Jesus or churches was strictly forbidden. I was told about the Jewish holidays.

The orphanage was on a lake and during the winter, I often went to school on ice skates. One day, when arriving at school, I remember a part of the school surrounded by a fence with strange and sick looking people inside. It was 1945 and the war had ended. A group of survivors of concentration camps had been placed there to recover and be resettled. I knew my parents had been put into a concentration camp but since my memory of my "original" home had been replaced by my new home at the Gustafsson's farm, I didn't even look through the fence to see if maybe I could find my parents.

After living at the orphanage a year, I once again was told I would be "moving" because it was being closed. So once again I packed the black suitcase and was put on a train, this time going north again, to a place called Stockholm, the capital of Sweden.

I have very little recollection of my year at the orphanage. I don't even remember a single name of my room mates nor was there ever a single letter from anyone. It became the place at which I would be reminded that I am Jewish and to forget about Christians.

The best I can say about the orphanage was that it was a place to live, have food to eat and a school. As such, it became another important event in my life learning how to deal with being disconnected from a family and friends, face unknowns and learning how to deal with sudden and dramatic change.

Stockholm
1945-1946

Again, I was sent away with my one black suitcase that contained all my worldly possessions. I am getting older, now 12 and at least knowing Swedish, my new language.

My new "foster family" was the "Jakob and Natalia Koffs. They had one son, Martin, who was in the Swedish army and lived in an apartment. The Koff's were a very religious family originally from Eastern Europe(Ukraine, I think) and very observant of Jewish laws. Friday night "Shabbat" with candle lighting, special dinners and yes, it's all "kosher".

This was a tremendous culture shock to me, I had finally become "at home" with the Gustafssons, a fundamental religious Christian family living in a small horse and buggy farm where you ate what you grew including milking cows and eating the pigs you raised.

The new world (for me) in Stockholm was dramatic because the food I had become familiar with on the Gustafsson farm was mostly what they grew on the farm, extremely "healthy, natural" and simple. The Koffs on the other hand kept strictly kosher which to me was greasy spoon Eastern European style "Yiddish" food. The transition and shock from basic farm living through an orphanage to a greasy spoon Eastern European Kosher life ruined my stomach forever. Having lived through ulcers, chronic gastritis and today, acid reflux probably originated with these severe gastric transitions.

Instead of living in horse & buggy style, I now lived in a large city with street cars, buses and cars. Except on the "Shabbat" (Saturday), when we all had to attend synagogue nearly across town, we had to walk because it was forbidden to "ride" in anything.

Since I was then 12 years old, I had to be sent to learn yet another very strange language, Hebrew". According to Jewish law, every 13 year old boy must "become "Bar Mitzvah" which is coming of age in the religion. I was sent to a school to learn this language of the bible and prepare for that special day when I was to become 'Bar Mitzvah" which happened March, 1946.

Herr Koff's business was making chandeliers made of expensive crystal. My job was to work in his factory stringing the crystals onto the chandeliers.

I learned a great deal in Stockholm. A lot about European history walking through Stockholm's "Gamla Stan" (old town) where the royal castle of the king lived and which was built in the 11th century, almost back to the time of the Vikings.

Then one day, I received a letter from a Ruth Krumbein who lived in a far away place called Pensacola, Florida in America. This excited me. I had heard about a new world called America where everyone was a millionaire. She invited me to come to America to live with her family and said she was my Father's half sister. Why shouldn't I go? I had no friends, didn't like the strict "Kosher" life style and really didn't know what would become of me. What did I have to lose? And, by this time, I had become somewhat used to facing unknowns.

So I said YES!. And so once again, my black suitcase was packed. Again with all my worldly possessions, still having the envelope with pictures from my parents and Germany, I was shipped off to off to America, a new world, a new language and once again, a world of strangers.

Since I knew no English at all, not even a word and realized I had to once again learn an entirely new language, now speaking only Swedish and having forgotten German, someone prepared for me an index card with ten basic words in Swedish translated into English. With this card, my black suitcase with the same pictures my mother had put in it, a "Letter" of credit for the ticket on the ship and letter with the address where I was being shipped, I was once again put on a train in Stockholm bound for yet a new world and new life.

Gunther shipped off to America
Departed Sweden July, 1946

I was put on a train in Stockholm, again alone, bound for Gothenburg on the Swedish west coast to board the MS Gripsholm, the ship that would take me to America. This time I was 13 years old and unlike the trip from Germany to Sweden seven years earlier when I was only six, I knew what was happening.

The M.S. Gripsholm, Swedish American Line, ship

Gunther crossed the Atlantic July-August, 1946. Gunther under the ship's bell. The Gripsholm was the first transatlantic ocean liner built(1926) since the Titanic went down 1912. The Gripsholm carried 1600 passengers in three classes, First, Tourist and "common".

These classes were segregated the First being on top, Tourist in the middle and "common" on bottom. Needless to say, I was in the "bottom" in a cabin with two bunk beds for four passengers.

I spent most of the time down in the cabin, sick, because there were constant storms in the North Sea and Northern Atlantic. Someone was nice to take a picture of me, the only picture of me on this ship.

Gripsholm lapel pin I still wear on my sport jacket. The "Three Crown" is the emblem of Sweden.

Arrived in New York
August 5, 1946

I arrived in New York alone, with that same black suitcase my parents had "shipped" me out with when I was forced to flee Germany just seven years before. Just as when arriving to Sweden, I faced a new world, new people and a new language I didn't understand nearly a word. But unlike when arriving to Sweden, I knew who I was, where I came from and thought I knew where I was going. I still have that passport(shown here) and have always kept a passport current just in case I had to again seek safety.

I had been allowed to come on a special Swedish Refugee Passport" under the U.S. German quota which was accepted by the U.S. Immigration officer as I disembarked. Once again, I had been "reborn" in a new world but this time I was "ready".

A Swedish speaking lady met me just as I came through the immigration line with an envelope and directions to where I was headed next. She took me to a hotel for the night as I was scheduled to leave on a train the following morning bound for a place called Pensacola, Florida" with an overnight in Atlanta.

The envelope contained train tickets and a letter I was to show people for help as I didn't know any English. The lady was from the Travelers Aid Society who told me I would be met by another Travelers Aid representative in Atlanta where I would spend the night and be put on another train for my final destination.

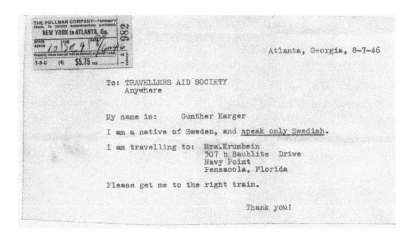

So here, I go from yet another train station(I think it was Pennsylvania Station in New York), with that same black suitcase from Germany containing all my worldly possessions. My next adventure in "the New World".

Gunther arrives in Pensacola
August 7, 1946

When the train arrived to a place called Flomaton, Florida, which was the place trains stopped for Pensacola, I was handed an envelope by the conductor with a note in Swedish telling me to get off.

When I got off the train, I felt like having arrived in hell. The wall of hot, humid air greeted me as did a short lady and man. Facing the hot, Gulf of Mexico steaming weather in August for the first time being used to the northern Europe climate was a shock. Had I known then what "hell' really awaited me and If I could have, I might have gotten back on that train and fled back to Sweden.

The situation of a 13 year old refugee not speaking English being met by a couple which knew no Swedish at all and a lady trying to communicate with me in German (which I had forgot) was a scene that should have been captured in the movies.

I think that was the moment which created serious problems between the husband of the lady meeting me and myself because apparently, me not being able to communicate with him meant I lacked intelligence. From that moment on through the four years I would live with this couple I had serious relational problems with the man who I was to call "Uncle Jack" and to a lesser extent with his wife who became "Aunt Ruth".

It seemed that my new 'foster parents" equated my inability to speak English and immediately communicate with me as being stupid. Ingrained into my memory are the many times "Uncle Jack" called me a "moron" never to be good for much and probably ending up in life as a farm hand.

What I didn't know because no one had ever told me was that this "Uncle Jack" and "Aunt Ruth" had just adopted an infant and were expecting me to become their servant.

Unlike the Gustafssons on the farm in Sweden where I was expected to work hard but always as a member of their family as they too worked hard, here in the "New World" I was treated as a slave and someone less than a "person"

Yes, I was given my own room in their house, food and clothes. But I also was required to change the diapers on their new adopted infant, wash the dishes, scrub the floors, mow the lawn and baby sit for them and their friends.

Two weeks after arriving, I was introduced to the owner of a supermarket across town and given a job as bag boy and shelf stocker being paid 25 Cents/hour. Although I was allowed to keep a small part of this for my allowance, most had to be given to my "foster parents". This continued for the entire four years I lived with "Aunt Ruth & "Uncle Jack". School, work at jobs and work in their house as a servant from age 13 to 17. I don't remember making a single "friend" during this time.

I was entered into the 7th grade at a junior high school, one year behind because I didn't know much English starting school only a few weeks after arriving. But I learned quickly and skipped the 8th grade because I made good grades and learned very quickly. The only person I remember from the four years of school in Pensacola was Mrs. Earnest who was the Spanish teacher.

My relationship with "Uncle Jack" was never good. I felt like the outsider in their home who was there only because Aunt Ruth had somehow tried to honor some promise to my father and I was useful as a servant. She had emigrated to the U.S. in the late 1930's from Berlin sponsored by a famous local Doctor whose wife was none other than "Frances Wolfson", sister of the famous "Mitchell Wolfson" who founded Wometco Enterprises of Miami, This was the company eventually owning the entertainment empire including Wometco Theatres, TV stations and the Sequarium of Key Biscayne, the home of "the "Flipper TV series" . I became the "servant" refugee boy from Europe who was a lot "less" than such "folk".

As time passed and I reached 17 years, our relationship became more and more difficult as I started to better understand the world and people for who and what they really are. I also realized that I had really no friends nor relatives who were concerned about me in any personal way.

Based on the norms of society as I have come to know and understand, if there were ever anyone subject to taking to drugs to escape reality or take to crime, to get even with the world, it probably was me. But no, I kept focused on getting through this troubled time of my life as quickly as possible, learning the most in school and from life around and becoming independent from others. I never took drugs, excessive drinks nor got in trouble with the police. I was too occupied "getting through" each day which to me became more "hell" than I ever had experienced, even being a Holocaust survivor.

Gunther Karger

Gunther thrown out!
Pensacola, Summer, 1950

School had just let out for the 1950 summer break with me finishing the 11th grade and I was 17 years old. I had just washed the car and was about to catch the bus to my job at the supermarket when "Uncle Jack" yelled out in a mean tone "You caused a flat tire, dumb bell. Go out and change the tire".

I guess the four years of demeaning put downs telling me I am no good had reached its limit as I responded "Go fuck yourself!". (in good English)

That ended my American experience in Pensacola because I was told to pack my suitcase (same black suitcase I fled Germany with) and be gone in the morning. That I did and would be ready to "go" in the morning. To where I had yet to find out and learned that evening.

One of my few remembrances I did have from Germany were Uncle Alfred's(my Mother's half brother) visits on his motorcycle with his wife, Aunt Elsa riding in the side car. I was told that evening that early the next morning, I would leave with all my belongings, never to come back and go to "Uncle Alfred" in New Jersey

He and his wife, aunt Elsa had been able to flee Germany to Montevideo, Uruguay(South America) in 1938 and had recently moved to New Jersey where they bought a chicken farm. Uncle Jack and Aunt Ruth decided to ship me off to their farm. They sent Uncle Alfred a Western Union telegram telling them that "Gunther" will be visiting them for a two week summer vacation and will be arriving by Greyhound Bus in a few days.

I managed to again pack my suitcase with all that I could bring, cleaned up "my room" and was put on the Greyhound bus early next morning. Next stop would be my 5th including four foster homes and one orphanage in two countries and continents. I swore to myself the "next" would be my last. The one worry I did have was how I would be able to finish high school.

Greyhound bus to New Jersey
Riding with dead passenger

This was to be a trip I would never forget. Not because I left "hell' but because of what happened on this trip.

The bus arrived into the Atlanta Greyhound station early in the morning while it was still dark. This time though, I wasn't waiting for a Travelers Aid person because now, my English was good and I could get about on my own.

I was sitting in the window seat and couldn't get out until the man sitting next got up. The problem was he didn't move and couldn't. He was dead. I had been sitting next to a dead person. After the police did its thing, all passengers could get off and I got on the bus to New Jersey where I would be met by "Uncle Alfred".

The Chicken Farm
Foster home No. Five
1950-1951

I got off the Greyhound bus as it pulled into the Philadelphia station and someone waved with a sign "Gunther". Uncle Alfred had changed his name from Alfred to Alfredo in South America and now had become "Fred" just as my name was changed from Günter(German) to "Gynter" in Sweden because in Swedish there is no "ü" and when I came to America, I became "Gunther".

Uncle Fred met me in Philadelphia instead of Vineland, New Jersey (about 30 miles south of Philadelphia) because he was in Philadelphia where his wife, Aunt Elsie (changed from Elsa to Elsie making name transitions from Germany to South America to the U.S.) had just the day before given birth to "Susan", their first child(Uncle Fred and Aunt Elsie were both about 45 years of age). They had just themselves started another "new life" in another country having fled Germany 1938 to Montevideo, Uruguay(South America, just next to Argentina). This was the very person who sometimes visited my home in Germany coming on his motorcycle with his wife, Elsie riding the side car. This was also the first time since I was forced to flee Germany that I had met anyone from my childhood in Germany which stirred my erased Germany memories.

"Why are you here with that large black suitcase from Germany? Isn't that too much for a two week vacation that your Uncle Jack mentioned in his telegram?" That became the moment I decided to again deal with reality by telling Uncle Fred the truth. I had been thrown out by the Krumbeins and could not return. I came on a one way bus ticket, needed a place to live for one more year until I graduated high school.

This became an event etched into my mind forever. A person who himself just came to the U.S. after fleeing the Nazis and spending 12 years in South America as a furniture polisher starting a new life on a chicken farm with a wife, age 45 in the hospital having their first baby suddenly facing a 17 year old rough looking boy getting off the bus with no place to go.

I made him this offer, right there and then at that bus station. "Could I live with his family, just for one year until I graduated high school if I worked on his chicken farm?" He said he would discuss it with his wife who just had a baby the day before and he was picking up at the hospital after picking me up at the bus station.

We left the bus station to pick up Aunt Elsie and their new daughter at the hospital and drove to their South Jersey farm not only with a new baby, but with a 17 year old boy who would live with them for a year.

I had survived yet another "crisis" and had entered yet another "New life" in yet another strange place with a new family. Since my parents sent me away from Germany and our ancestral home to "live another day", this new place in New Jersey would make it for me four foster homes and one orphanage in two countries in two continents making transitions including learning two totally different languages "cold turkey".

I had survived "to live another Day". Despite having survived the ordeal just two days before sitting next to a dead person on the Greyhound bus in Atlanta. I had "survived" being literally "thrown out" by a foster family in Florida after being kept as a virtual slave for four years. I was getting to be an experienced "survivor" having learned the necessity to face and deal with dramatic and sudden changes.

Gunther on the Chicken Farm

Gunther in front of the chicken coops

Uncle Fred(Alfred became "Fred"), and aunt Elsie's chicken farm was on Tuckahoe Rd in Newfield, New Jersey about 30 miles south of Philadelphia midway to Atlantic City and just north of Vineland. The farm consisted of a small house with a large cellar and several long chicken coups where thousands of chickens were sitting on racks laying eggs.

The cellar under the house was where the eggs were sorted out with a "grading machine" where eggs were classified according to size and put into cartons. Although my main job was to collect the eggs in the coops, I also was the coop cleaner. Aunt Elsie said that I was the fastest egg collector she had ever seen but kept telling me to slow down because I also broke more eggs in the process of collecting them. Why? Because I had to hold my breath running through the chicken coops.The stench was as bad as you can imagine any smell to be and a gas mask wasn't available.

The chickens sat on the racks and dropped their shit to the ground where It accumulated until it piled up and had to be removed. Uncle Fred had a deal with a local chicken manure person to buy it for fertilizer processing. My job was to go into the bottom of the chicken coop with boots and shovel the chicken shit out and load it onto the truck.

Cleaning out chicken shit from chicken coops was the worst job I had ever had and probably would ever have. But that was the deal I had made with Uncle Fred. He let me live and gave me all that I needed…food, clothing and all plus the chance to finish high school on the condition that I help out on his farm.

Uncle Fred and Aunt Elsie treated me nice and for that I am forever grateful. While my previous foster parents treated me like a worthless slave telling me I would never amount to more than a farm hand. Uncle Fred and Aunt Elsie treated me as part of their family even though I was working on their farm. This chapter in my life prepared me for any job that might come along because cleaning chicken coops may be the worst job in the world and that was the job I had.

Alfred and Elsie Offer(Offenheimer) originally of Mannheim, Germany and fled Hitler's Germany to Uruguy before settling in New Jersey. They had two daughters, Susan and Evelyn

Clayton High School–New Jersey
1950-1951

For my last year in high school, I went to Clayton High School in Clayton, NJ about 10 miles from the chicken farm. The Senior Class had only 55 students. Even though they were from local lifelong families and I was the outsider, the teachers and students were nice to me. I made friends with one in particular, Bernie Rudberg whose parents came from Sweden and invited me sometimes to his house where I could speak Swedish with his folks. We keep in touch with him to this day summer, 2014).

Clayton High School was the first place my apparent speaking and organizing talent was discovered as I was invited to be a panelist on the "Student Townhall of the Air" program put on by WCAU, the Philadelphia TV station. I also ran for the vice president of my class and won.

Despite working always on the chicken farm, I paid attention to my school work because I had never forgotten the dream I had during my early days in Sweden to become a scientist working with space and rockets. I was making good grades and even elected to the National honor Society and given awards in mathematics.

In the spring of 1951, my senior class was preparing for its senior trip to Washington, DC, the nations capitol. The students raised money for this by doing various projects but Uncle Fred paid my share. That trip gave me insight into the American government and its history which was to become a huge factor in my life to come. Visits to the White House, Capitol, Lincoln Memorial, Smithsonian Institute and on the return, the U.S. Naval Academy at Annapolis inspired me because I then realized I had arrived at my "New Country".

Goodbye foster homes & orphanages
My 18th Birthday, March 16, 1951

As I was nearing my 18th birthday when I would finally become responsible for myself in all respects, the question arose "Where would I go? What would I do and how would I make a living?

I knew I needed to go to school somewhere to learn science and eventually get a job. Who would help pay for college? I had no parents, no family sponsorship nor any real friends who would look after me. Once again, I faced the world. Again alone, dependent only on myself.

I turned to my high school home room teacher, Anthony Galligani and my math teacher, Miss Pagano for advice. They helped me get scholarships to Drexel Institute of Technology and Rutgers University to get a degree in electrical engineering. But these were only partial scholarships and even if I got a part time job while going to school, it wouldn't be enough to pay tuition, room & board and all living expenses. And, as by now you already know, I have no family to help with anything.

I found my answer in the Korean War which was raging and the military was looking for soldiers. I learned that if you signed up for four years in the military, you were given a place to live, food to eat, doctors to help you keep well and most important of all, opportunity to go to schools. The military was the answer.

The U.S. Air force had just been separated from the Army to become its own military force and was looking for recruits to go to school learning how to do all kinds of jobs. That was my answer. Join the Air Force which would get me away from the stinking chicken coops and finally into a life where I would be in charge of myself and no longer be subject to being "shipped" around the world to live with strangers.

My new high school friend, Bernie, had a car and took me to the Air Force recruiting station in Woodbridge. The sergeant told me there were openings in aircraft radar but that I had to report for duty almost right away to go to basic training before I could even start any technical school. I also had to take the Air Force entrance test to qualify not only for the radar school, but to get into the Air Force. He offered me the opportunity to take the test right there and then, took it and passed. The next question? When do you want to sign up? I was just 18 and could join that day. But it was March and I wouldn't graduate high school until June.

I went to my school principal and told him of my dilemma and asked if there is any way for me to immediately take my end of High School tests and graduate before actually finishing the classes and if I passed all the tests, I could graduate without attending the graduation ceremony. The principal knowing of my unique circumstances and that my grades were tops, checked with my teachers and all agreed to my proposal.

I took my tests, passed them all with top grades and told everyone goodbye. Uncle Fred and aunt Elsie wished me well and on May 18, 1951, I caught the bus to Woodbury, N.J. and joined the Air Force. This trip would be different from any other trips. I had to leave the black suitcase behind because the Air force would supply most of my needs including uniforms. Uncle Fred agreed to keep the black suitcase and the violin which I still had from the church in Sweden.

I was finally a free person after enduring what no young person should be asked to endure at a young age. But, I had learned the basic lesson of life "If there is a will, there is a way" and I had yet again found "the way".

"My son, let them not depart from your eyes. Keep sound wisdom and discretion. Then, you will walk safely in your way and your foot will not stumble"
The Holy Bible, Proverbs

Gunther Karger

My 50th High School Reunion, 2001
(flash forward)

Before continuing with "Gunther's Story" and the next chapter starting with his Air Force career, let's "borrow Jules Verne's "Time Machine" and flash forward 25 years to learn what happened at Gunther's High School reunion 1976.

One of my high school classmates, Ruth Costa (now Stewart) had somehow tracked me down and begged me to come to the 25th reunion of our senior High School class. It was to be a weekend long event at a hotel in Vineland, NJ. The graduating class had been about 55 with about 50 attending the reunion including husbands and wives.

Greeting us at the "banquet" was a sign "Welcome back Gunther, our class Valedictorian". To my surprise, I had become declared "Valedictorian" in absentia resulting from my graduation having taken the final exams and didn't know. My former class mates asked me to say a few words about what happened to me since one day I was in school and the next day I was gone. They also remembered I had suddenly showed up from nowhere to start the senior year and thought it strange that I should also so suddenly disappear before the graduation.

To this day in July, 2014 as I am writing this book, I am still keeping up with classmates Ruth Costa and Bernie Rudberg. Bernie retired from IBM and just finished restoring the old Hopewell Railway Station in Fishkill, NY (along the Hudson River) as a museum.

U.S Air Force
May, 1951 – May, 1955

My first stop in the Air Force was Sampson Air Force Base located on the north tip of Lake Seneca in upstate New York just south of Rochester. I was on a bus full with other recruits. On arrival, we were told to get off, line up in a formation, meet our squadron sergeant, be assigned to our barracks and issued uniforms.

During the following 11 weeks of "Air Force boot camp, I learned not only about military life but also a new life on my own. I learned how to use weapons like rifles, hand gun, endurance tests and most of all, the need to stay focused on a mission. I even received the "Marksman Ribbon" for being a good shooter.

There isn't much more to say except that the Air Force and its boot camp was my window to life on my own. I had arrived to my own world.

When my squadron graduated Air Force basic training, everyone was sent to our respective specialist training. Since I had been assigned to become a specialist in airborne electronics, I was sent to Scott Air Force Base in Illinois, just across the Mississippi River east of St. Luis.

On arrival, there was a call for volunteer to run the base pool hall until classes started. I raised my hand and, for the following 6 weeks, I was in charge of the base pool hall playing pool and ping pong. One day, I was ordered to pack my bags and report to the flight line for school assignment.

There were several schools open for new classes and when the "Airborne Radar " at Keesler AFB was announced, I raised my hand. The sergeant told me to break out of formation and report with my duffel bag to the waiting DC – 3.

The DC-3 became my first airplane experience flying from Scott AFB in Illinois to Keesler AFB in Biloxi Miss. For those who may not remember this airplane, it was developed in the 1930's as American Airlines first big passenger plane carrying up to 30 passengers. About 10,000 were produced for commercial and military use with some still operating today. I show this plane because it was my first to fly and aviation became a big part of my life. It wasn't the space ship I had dreamt about in the Swedish Capt. Frank and Buck Rogers comic strips but it did get me off the ground.

Keesler AFB–Air Force School

I landed at the Keesler Air Base, August 1951. If you ever wondered what hell is like, try landing on a hot airfield anywhere on the upper Gulf Coast in August mid day. It was like landing inside an oven. The heat, humidity and mosquitos were unbearable especially if you wear a full uniform instead of shorts and a tee shirt.

We were all welcomed by an Air Force sergeant and marched in formation to an un-airconditioned wooden barracks which would be my home for the next nine months. My space in the barracks was a metal bunk bed with a mattress and a footlocker at the end of the bed and a cardboard like wardrobe for a closet to hang a few clothes. Yes, there was a fan somewhere moving a little air. There was a latrine on the end with common urinal, shower and a few sinks. For the others, this would be their "home away from their home" but for me, this would be my only home.

My squadron was assigned to attend the "Airborne Fundamentals Electronics School", where we would learn all about electronics and how such relates to airplanes. This basically was a four year college electrical engineering course compressed into nine months focused only on the essential things applicable to electronic fundamentals with the humanities and play removed.

We were assigned to the night shift which meant that we were marched to dinner at 11 pm and class at midnight. School was out at 5:00 am when we all were marched to the chow hall for breakfast and then back to the barracks to sleep by 6:00 am.

We were "off" weekends but then had other duties like cleaning the barracks and doing base maintenance. Yes, we were issued "off base" passes but that was almost meaningless because Biloxi had been placed "off limits" to military personnel.

Biloxi was declared too corrupt with bars, whorehouses and illegal gambling. This was way before the casinos arrived to Biloxi and a time when the 'sheriff" was in charge of all that was declared bad instead of the sheriff charged with getting rid of it.

We all were encouraged to use the USO for entertainment and yes, there was a roller rink in a nearby town to the east called Ocean City where "available" girls were known to be "trolling".

When I graduated from the nine month electronic fundamentals school, I was assigned to the six month specialist "Airborne Radar and Navigation" school to learn all about how such things worked and how to repair them. This was to become the somewhat famous "APQ13 Radar" and APN 9 Loran Navigation systems" course. The classes included lectures and working with the actual airborne equipment in the classroom and in the aircraft.

Gunther–The adventurous Innovator

Gradually becoming known as the person with new ways of doing things which I called better and more efficient, I became known as the creator of the "killer test". This was still the day of vacuum tubes, large electronic components like transformers, resistors and condensers big enough to see and feel, unlike today's microchips. The APQ-13 was a radar system consisting of several black boxes including the "Modulator" and the magnetron transmitter which sent a very high energy electromagnetic pulse to the antenna via rectangular metal pipes called waveguides.

A common equipment failure was the modulator putting out a low voltage trigger pulse to the transmitter. The voltage output modulator was a very high 12,000 volt high energy pulse from a specially ceramic insulated tip at the top of an oil cooled cylindrical metal can which looked like a miniaturized nuclear reactor. The prescribed procedure was to hook up special high test equipment capable of determining if the proper energy and voltage was being delivered to the transmitter.

This test took time setting it up hooking up test equipment. Not wanting to "waste time" because some of our proficiency tests were timed, I found a better way that took at most 5 minutes and didn't need any test equipment. The modulator tip at the proper 12000 volts would issue a strong blue large spark if near any metal. A weak output pulse would issue a yellow spark, The new and more efficient test system I created was to get a long screwdriver with a wooden handle, wrap a handkerchief or dry rag around the screwdriver handle, remove the top modulator connector insulator cap and turn the power on.

The final part of this test was to take the screwdriver with the handkerchief wrapped around the handle in one hand with the other hand in your pocket and very slowly move the metal tip of the screwdriver toward the modulator output tip which now is exposed. If there is no spark, the modulator is bad. If the spark is yellow or any color other than strong deep blue, it is putting out low voltage and needs to be repaired. But if the spark is a strong deep blue and can be heard, the modulator is properly operating at 12,000 volts.

When my instructor heard of my newly developed "test" he asked me to demonstrate it and told me that if I ever did this again, I would be dismissed form the class unless I first killed myself. He explained that what I was doing was using a manmade lighting strike to test equipment and he didn't want dead students. But he acknowledged that my new test did demonstrate my extraordinary understanding of the principles of electricity.

I included this test because it illustrates my uncanny ability to find simple more efficient ways to solve complex problems.

Radar can be deadly

Today we use microwaves for everyday cooking with wives knowing nothing about how the cooking is actually done. I remember one event which illustrates the potential dangers of working with and using microwaves.

Although I was assigned to the airborne electronics and radar school, Keesler also had a ground radar school. Ground radars were the very large systems used for long range aircraft and missile detection and on the civilian side, air traffic control. One day, a student had climbed inside the antenna of such radar system to check its microwave feedhorn. The operator in the control room didn't check if anyone was outside in the antenna area and hit the 'transmit" button. This sent a high power microwave beam right through the student's head cooking his brain just like you would have made popcorn in the microwave oven. Needless to say that the student in the control room's goose was also "cooked" and served at the other student's funeral reception.

Adventure in New York City

It's said that some good can come out of bad things. While "enslaved" with "Uncle Jack & Aunt Ruth" in Pensacola, my first "stop" in America after arriving from Sweden in 1946, I met "Uncle Jack's" two brothers. Aaron Krumbein of Chicago who was my best man in my wedding and Maurice Krumbein (famous band leader "Ray Carter"). They felt sorry for a kid seemed lost and always were nice to me.

When the Air Force school closed down for the Christmas holidays and the personnel all went home to be with their families, I had no home to visit. But Maurice who lived in NYC invited me and I went.

The problem was that I had no car so I made a deal with two other guys going to New York(their home) and went with them as one had a car. As we were driving through North Florida, infamous for sheriffs stopping cars in speed traps(still there), we got nailed by a local sheriff for speeding. We were forced to follow the police to a small grocery station where the store owner also was the local judge. The grocery store owner declared "Court in Session" and fined the driver of our car $50. We could either pay or go to the local jail(in back of the store) for one day. We all chipped in and "bailed out". I was dropped off at Maurice's apartment in Forest Hills for a week and picked up for the drive back to Keesler. Maurice's family was real nice to me.

Maurice also was "Ray Carter" the famous big band leader who did music for radio and TV shows. He invited me to the Arthur Murray TV show for which his band did the live music. In case you have forgotten, Arthur Murray and his wife, Kathryn Murray were the hosts of that show and creators of the famous nationwide Arthur Murray Dance Studio". During the show, I was introduced to the famous pop singer Teresa Brewer who appeared as guest on that particular show and I got to dance with Kathryn Murray(in my Air Force uniform).

Their daughter, Judith, was a violin student at Julliard School of Music (probably the most famous music school in America). She took me round town and introduced me to Chinese food at the House of Chan near Times Square and "Brandy Alexander"

I mention this "episode" as there will be more throughout this book telling of my constant flight from the dark depths of my personal Holocaust eventually taking me to the White House on one assignment, meeting Dr. Wernher von Braun, the famous German rocket scientist and many more noted people. I already had graduated far higher than the best "Uncle Jack" had told me I would become that being a "farm hand".

Gunther Karger

Here come the New Orleans Girls
Shirley, September, 1951

The night shift at Keesler left only weekends for other things. The base chaplain had put up a notice about some Jewish girls from New Orleans coming to the Biloxi USO with bagels and lox. I was kind of a loner, had no girlfriends "back home" (no home to go back to) and was ready to face at least some kind of social challenge. So I went. What's to lose? When you have little or nothing to lose, why not "go for it"?

The USO was on a pier reaching out on the Biloxi beach east of town. When I got there, there were a bunch of nice looking girls sitting in chairs along a wall. Music was playing and what the heck, I went to one of them to ask for a dance. No go. She said 'you are too short. it's true that I'm only 5' 5" but then, good things come in small packages. She also said, but here is my sister who is shorter.

Her sister was Shirley with whom I today have been married 60 years. She was the girl who rescued a guy who came from nowhere, no family and nothing.

The "New Orleans girls" came in on a bus from New Orleans and were sponsored by "BBG of New Orleans". "BBG" stands for B'nai Brith Girls" which is a Jewish girls organization. Apparently there was a shortage in New Orleans where parents were anxious for their daughters to meet Jewish guys.

The fishing expedition to the Keesler Air Base USO actually worked out well. Eventually, at least a half dozen of the girls on that bus found their "dream Air Force Guy" and got married, including myself. Some of the guys also got lucky and got jobs for life as they were taken into the girls family business. One of the girls was the daughter of the owner of the famous restaurant 'Court of Two Sisters" in the middle of French Quarter". Over the years, we kept in touch with most of them. They remain married as of this book being written and the guy is now the owner. Another girl came with a house her parents gave them when they got married.

Me? I just got Shirley and found a new family in the land of opportunity – America. We will celebrate our 60th anniversary with the release of this book.

Shirley at 16   Our engagement in 1953

Gunther – The Air Force Instructor

When I graduated the airborne radar school(1952), I was offered and accepted the opportunity to stay at Keesler to be assigned to the Air Force Technical Training Command as "Technical Instructor".

This led me yet to another school "The Air Force Instructor School" which turned out to be a really good decision. Given my troubled background, having to learn two totally different languages, making transition to multiple cultures and basically being a loner, this offered me the opportunity to improve my communication skills.

This school taught personal communication, speaking and presentation skills which would become extremely helpful over my entire life. Facing having to stand in front of my first class for me was like a chicken breaking out of its shell. From that moment on, I had no problems speaking before groups later in life even becoming a speaker on major cruise ships and at conventions.

One incident worth noting herein is how I handled a student who insisted sleeping in my class because he believed that he learned more asleep than awake. Many students were seasoned Air Force career people who came to school for recurrent training and eligibility to higher jobs. I was a young person looking even younger than I actually was (still have the same problem at age 81). This led to resentment by some students who had problems with learning anything from anyone younger them themselves. This was the problem with the "sleeper"

So I offered the "sleeper" a deal. He could sleep for one test period if he agreed to keep awake for a second. If his test grades were better after the "sleeping period" than when he kept awake and were at least passing, I would let him sleep in class. Although he made better grades while asleep, he failed and also failed while being awake. I flunked him out of school and he went back to the "line" demoted one grade.

Gunther the weatherman

Since the days of Buck Rogers, I had continued to be focused on space reading science fiction thinking I would be someday working in that business exploring the unknown. So it was a natural yes when I was offered the opportunity to be one of the three person team to set up the Air Force's first weather training school for weather forecasting using the radar I was already teaching for airborne operations.

So off I went to Chanute AFB in central Illinois where the Air Force Meteorological School was training Air Force personnel to become weather forecasters and maintenance of weather equipment. I was assigned to a much nicer living quarter than at Keesler where I still lived in a wooden barracks. This was a four story building with individual rooms of two persons per room.

My room mate was a guy from Iowa, Gene Kirchner with whom I became friends lasting to this day. Shirley & I visited him and his family in Bakersfield, Calif on one of our many trips to California. Gene was interested in science and space like me and when he left the air Force, he became an astronomy and physics professor at Bakersfield College in California.

The meteorology (weather) school taught me all there is to learn about the weather, cloud formations and all the equipment used In weather forecasting. While we were going to the weather school, my team also started configuring the aircraft radar as ground based weather forecasting system.

When my team finished setting up the new weather radar course and took the first class through it, I was offered the opportunity to return back to Keesler in Mississippi for the advanced senior level airborne radar and navigation school. This was great because Shirley & I had been corresponding and I could get back to the "New Orleans girls.

My Chicago Adventure

I would be remiss not mentioning my Chicago adventure before returning to Keesler and Mississippi.

While still living with the Koff family in Stockholm, Sweden, I had met the Sinofsky family who emigrated to Chicago. They learned that I was living in Illinois and invited me to spend one of the Jewish holiday with them.

Since I didn't have a car, I hitchhiked the 300 miles north on the highway which could have turned out as a disaster. One car stopped to pick me up (I wore the uniform). When they started to pass the whiskey bottle around, I decided to bolt and left at the next gas stop.

This was to be one of my several trips to Chicago and I'll cite one memory which becomes part of my religious journey. Born Jewish, sent to live with deeply religious Christian farmers and then on to super religious observant Jews in Stockholm and then to the Krumbeins of Florida who were reformed Jews believing that orthodox Jews were low class people left a mark on me. I will deal with this in a later chapter where I address my views on religion.

A rule for observant Jews is not to "work" on the Sabbath which starts at sundown Friday ending sunset Saturday. The extreme observance means not to drive a car, go shopping, answer the phone and of course, not work at any job. The Sinofsky's were very observant especially their father who also came with the family from Sweden. He was sort of a rabbi who killed chickens the kosher way and saying the proper prayer in that process.

But he also smoked cigarettes and this became a problem because it was against the rule to light a cigarette with a lighter or match on the Sabbath. This problem was solved by lighting one jet on the kitchen gas stove before sunset on Fridays or Jewish holidays which was used to light cigarettes. Another problem was the TV. It was OK to watch TV so long it had been turned on before sundown but not OK to turn it off and then turn it back on Saturday during the day because it then was still the Sabbath.

This problem was solved by a mechanical one trip timer which turned off the TV Friday night and paying a kid on the street (paying before sundown on Friday) a quarter to come to the apartment to turn on the TV Saturday mornings.

This added to my ongoing religious questioning which was accumulating in my mind as I became exposed to such radically different religious practices. Look for my views on religion in the section of this book where I express my thoughts on religion and its impact on the world.

Gunther averts airplane disaster

When I went to high school in Pensacola, I did meet one girl, Bonnie and corresponded with her occasionally during succeeding years. Her family moved to Milwaukee and when Bonnie invited me for a visit, I scheduled my vacation for a visit to Milwaukee. It had been several years since we saw each other and she had grown taller and said I needed to go to the shoe store to get elevator shoes before she would attend a dance with me.

The next morning I said my farewell to Bonnie and hopped on a bus to Mitchell Air Base in Milwaukee to hitch a ride to New Orleans and Shirley for whom I was not too short.

The airplane I was able to get on was a C-74 cargo plane bound for Tinker AFB in Oklahoma City. This was still the era of propeller planes and prop planes couldn't fly over the high storms in the Midwest. As we approached Oklahoma, we faced a line of strong storms with tops exceeding 40,000 ft. forcing the pilot to fly directly through the storm at about 25,000 ft. As we approached the storm, the sky got dark with wind rocking the plane. It eventually got pitch black except when lighting flashed all around the plane and hail hitting the windshield.

Then, lightning struck the plane forcing the pilot to shut down one engine as sparks were seen coming from it and he had to also shut down the engine on other side for balance so the plane now was flying on two engines in the midst of a really bad storm. Another lightning strike shut down the radio altimeter leaving only the barometric altimeter functioning. That was dangerous because in the midst of such storms, the barometric pressure can drop significantly giving wrong altitude readings for the pilot and you don't know how high the plane is flying. So, me being an avionics technician and instructor got out the emergency cockpit toolbox and went to work trying to fix the radio altimeter so the pilot wouldn't run into a high hill.

Obviously, since I am still "here" to write this book, the plane made it to the air base in Oklahoma City. But, I didn't wait for a plane to New Orleans. I went on the road and hitchhiked all the 600 miles to New Orleans where Shirley was still waiting for me. A close call it was.

The Supply sergeant

One of the more striking memories of Chanute AFB was the story of Sergeant Giles who was the squadron's supply sergeant. He was a big, burly cigar smoking beer drinker who always bragged about his juicy sex before breakfast with his wife. One day, when he apparently was really energetic after his juicy breakfast, he was driving on U.S. Hwy 45 along the railroad track. He wanted to prove he could outrun the freight train by getting to the rail crossing ahead of the locomotive. Tragically, his Lincoln didn't make it as the locomotive hit his car just as he was crossing the tracks. He would never know that I never forgot him and now with this book, he'll become immortalized because he challenged the locomotive with his big Lincoln and lost the "Battle of the Track".

How I became U.S. Citizen

I came to the U.S. under a European refugee passport issued by Sweden under the German Quota. This allowed me entry with permanent residence status including authorization to apply for citizenship. However, I had to wait until I was 18 to apply for Citizenship under the 'Declaration to apply for citizenship" which I filed promptly when reaching 18. This would allow me to actually receive my citizenship status five years later.

One day when arriving to the school entrance, the guard denied my entry and escorted me to the security office. I was told that I could not return to work until I get my security clearance which just had been revoked. Why? Because I was not a citizen and citizenship status was required for my clearance level. However, If I immediately file a declaration that I am in the armed service on active duty, the five year wait would be waived and I would be scheduled for an expedited citizenship hearing before a U.S. District judge. This court hearing occurred January 28, 1954 in U.S. District court in Danville, Il.

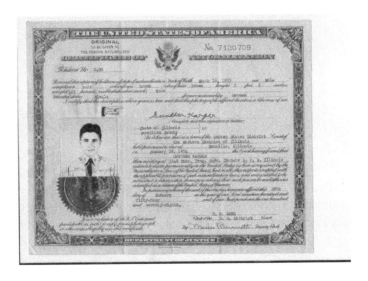

Return to Keesler AFB and the New Orleans Girls

I had been offered the opportunity to return to Keesler AFB in Mississippi for the advanced level Airborne Radar and Navigation school and grabbed it. This would take me closer to a career in airborne and space technology and back to the New Orleans girls and Shirley.

I returned to Keesler (Biloxi) in spring 1954 and when the course was finished in December the same year, we got married in New Orleans on December 5, 1954 on my way back to Illinois where my assignment in the weather radar school would continue. Below is my graduating class in the Senior advanced Air Force Radar school at Keesler.

We also decided(it now became "we" instead of "I") to leave the Air Force after the conclusion of my four year commitment and then go to Louisiana State University (LSU) where I had been accepted into its Electrical Engineering School. I could afford that thanks to the Government Veterans program.

Gunther & Shirley's wedding 12/5/1954

**Our wedding
New Orleans, Louisiana December 5, 1954**

The lone war refugee from Europe marries into a large New Orleans family and is alone no more.

Shirley Rosenzweig Karger
December 5, 1954
Born September 27, 1934

This was a unique wedding. Shirley had a large family with aunts, uncles, and lots of friends. Not to slight anyone for not being invited, everybody was invited and about 500 people came. All except two people were from Shirley's side since I had no family. The two from my side was myself, the groom and the other Aaron Krumbein, "Uncle Jack's " brother who also was my best man. We had actually invited the Krumbeins, despite our problems but they didn't come.

The question arises: How could Shirley's family afford a wedding of 500 people including everyone being invited to the reception? It was a "pot luck" wedding with many people bringing their own food. The bread delivery man brought bread, bakery owner cakes and desserts and the milkman brought milk and cream for the coffee. The liquor store owner down the street brought the drinks and so it went. Shirley saved up working for the wedding gown and me? I just brought myself, the groom who made all this possible. And I was the groom from nowhere…not the lawyer, doctor or son of store owners.

Me, I brought just myself but barely so because I almost didn't make the wedding. On the way driving from Keesler with all my stuff in the car to the New Orleans wedding, I got pulled over by a cop and given a ticket. Since the cop saw I was moving and unlikely to either pay the ticket or appear in court, he arrested me and took me to the police station threatening to keep me in jail until I paid the ticket. So I paid with what was almost all the cash I had and took off for New Orleans with all my stuff in the car. Yes, I still had that black suitcase from Germany but now, I had a few more things.

And I no longer was alone. From now on, it would be "Shirley & me" facing the world together, The long "ride" started and as of this writing, it's lasted 60 years.

Our wedding gave us a good start. While the episode on the way to the wedding depleted my cash to almost nothing, money we got as wedding presents was more than enough to get us to Illinois and look for an apartment.

Some of the gifts we received such as the pot and pan set from "aunt Frieda" has lasted us to this day. Shirley still makes her now famous chicken soup in the large pot aunt Frieda gave us. Aunt Frieda was Jennie Grossman's mom and Shirley's good friend. Jennie's husband, Jacob owned a liquor store in New Orleans who was shot and killed in an armed robbery.

My First Cars

My first car was a 1938 Chevvy coupe I bought for $75 while at Keesler just before going to Mobile, Alabama(about 60 miles away) for a weekend. I bought it the day before leaving but on the way late night, it broke down in the middle olf nowhere. I slept til the morning and then hitchiked back to Keesler, leaving the car by the side of the road, never again seeing it.

1938 Chevvy Coupe 1940 Ford V8

My second car bought in Illinois at Chanute AFB was a 1940 Ford V8. That was a great car but since it used a lot of oil, I traded it in for a 1949 Mercury before moving back to Biloxi. But it used too much oil also so I took it back to the used car dealer who gave me a case of "Staboil" which is a heavy 90 weight oil that plugs up the engine stopping leaks. That heavy oil worked for the 3 years I had the car. The Merc was the car I drove to the wedding and shirley & I traveled together to illinois in the dead of winter in December, 1954.

Our first six months- Illinois

Immediately after our wedding, we got into our1949 Mercury car already packed with all our belongings and took off for Chanute AFB in Rantoul, Ill. This was the first time Shirley would live away from her parents and New Orleans.

Our first stop was the Melrose Motel outside New Orleans which started our life journey that as of today has reached 60 years. The next morning we drove north 700 miles toward the freezing winter of central Illinois. This would be our "honeymoon".

Before reporting in for duty at Chanute AFB, we found our first place to live. A one bedroom attic apt. in Champaign, Ill. It really was in the attic of a lady's house. Since the bedroom had no windows, I drew a picture of a window on the wall.

I reported to my duties and resumed teaching at the Air Force weather school. Shirley looked for a job and got one at Eisners Supermarket main office as a keypunch operator in its book keeping dept, despite never having done that nor knowing anything about book keeping. Her supervisor, Mary Ellison fell in love with Shirley, taught her all about keypunching. I will never forget our first visitor to the apartment when Mary came with her two girls with an Easter basket wearing Easter bonnets. The image of this sight will forever be etched in our minds. Shirley corresponded with Mary for several years after we left Illinois but unfortunately she succumbed to cancer.

The six months in Illinois passed with us getting used to snow, ice and freezing weather and ended when I was discharged May 18, 1955 after my four years in the Air Force. During this time, I had found my own life away from foster homes, orphanages and become an aircraft electronics instructor and a wife. Basically, the Air Force to me became my portal to a new life. I had once again been reborn!.

LSU, Baton Rouge, La.
1955-1958

The next stop was Louisiana State University, Baton Rouge and on the way to becoming an electrical engineer. I was on my way to the space dream I had reading the science fiction comic strip years earlier in Sweden. To realize such a dream, I had to learn much more about science and the university offered that opportunity.

I picked LSU for several reasons. It offered a broadly based engineering education giving me knowledhe not only of electrical engineering which was the program I chose, but many of the related scientific disiplines such as astronomy, physics, chemistry, fluid dynamics and especially mathematics. The program I chose actually gave me a major in math and that's important not only in science and the understanding of the universe, but also in business as well.

I was able to structure a schedule wherein a full four year program became compressed into less than three years. This was made possible by taking a heavy class schedule, going to summer school two of the three summers and being extremely focused on the studies. I also was able to receive some credits for the many Air Force schools I had attended. The final summer I was able to get a "summer job with IBM where I learned a great deal about computers.

Another reason I picked LSU was that the cost fell within my means reflecting the GI educational benefits for veterans and Shirley would be working as I went to school.

LSU had available housing for veterans at a very low cost of $32 per month including even utilities. We were able to get this for the last of the three years we were at LSU. These quarters called "The Huts" were nothing more than wooden crates raised up on stilts above the ground. The crates had been used in WW II to tranport aircraft engines. The first year, we rented a small efficiently apt at 267 Lovers Lane, Honeymoon Apt. No 2. We had no financial help from anyone and there was no student loan then.

Although the Huts were within sight of famed Tiger Stadium on campus, I not even once attended a football game despite being there during the famed 1958 season when the LSU Tigers were champions of college football. My focus was studies, becoming a good electrical engineer and getting a job so we could make a good living.

I did encounter some difficulty resulting from still residual discrimination by some faculty, this being a "Southern University". In one instance for example, my test scores were frequently lower than my fellow class mates and when I questioned the professor on this, his response was that he knew the other students knew the subject but that I didn't necessarily know it. Instead of challenging such practice, I simply worked harder to avoid wasting time complaining because I was grateful having the opportunity of a great education.

Shirley had several jobs working at Floyd Electric in the book keeping dept but wasn't a great book keeper. So she got jobs as secretary in Governor Long's office at the State Capitol and in the Dean of Entomology (bugs) at LSU. She worked nearly the entire time at LSU and even though she made only about $25 per week, that helped us get through college.

Air Traffic Control Computer Summer Job, IBM 1957

I was offered a summer job in 1957 between my junior and senior college years by IBM at its Kingston, NY laboratory. This is the place where an IBM SAGE computer was being used to create the first large scale air traffic control computer. The SAGE computer was the "Semi Automatic Ground Environment" computer which started being used in the mid 50's as part of the country's detection of unfriendly aircraft and ICBM's entering American air space. This computer was being used by the NORAD (North American Air Defense) inside Cheyenne Mountain at Colorado Springs.

I was assigned to help develop high speed magnetic core memory which later (1959) led me to the Bell Labs in New Jersey where I was assigned to help develop memories operating at near absolute zero temperature which is minus 459 degrees Fahrenheit. In case you don't know what happens at this extremely low temp, the resistance of conducting wires theoretically goes to zero thereby allowing extremely fast data transfer which is critical in computers requiring the processing of high data at extreme speeds.

While I seem to be a target for difficult assignments, I have learned to reach for the unknown because it's always been my belief that the greatest challenge and risk for mankind lies in "what we don't know" and especially space where the greatest unknown exists. This is the reason why I believe President Obama made one of his biggest mistakes when he cancelled the American Manned Space Program in 2010. Instead, he should have reached out to other nations to create an international manned space program which would have stimulated the world economy at a time when its economy was collapsing and encouraging cooperation which could have reduced world terrorism. More on this later in this book.

While in Kingston, we rented a studio apt. in the home of Frau (Mrs) Zimmer (a German widow). Frau (she preferred to be called "Frau") Zimmer came to love Shirley and we kept in touch till her death years later.

Also while in Kingston, Shirley started to not feel well which we learned after returning to LSU in the fall of 1957 was because she had become pregnant. This being totally unexpected, I tracked back how such could have happened and I blamed the chickens for it. We had visited Uncle Alfred on the chicken farm in New Jersey one weekend and we were kept awake one night by cackling chickens.

We returned after the end of summer 1957 to LSU for my final year at the university. By this time, we had graduated to a 1953 Oldsmobile and were becoming already experienced travelers. A far cry from the "black suitcase war refugee".

1953 Oldsmobile Holiday Coupe

Graduated LSU 1958

Spring 1958 was an important milestone in our lives. I was about to graduate university (LSU) and had to decide which job to take and where we would live. The "we" had changed from just Shirley & me to us with our new baby, Herbert(named for my father). The picture below is "us" on my graduation and ready for whatever lay ahead.

I was lucky to have received seven job offers each including paying for our moving to wherever they were located. By now, I was not only a graduate electrical engineer, but also someone who had not only graduated several top Air Force schools, but actually worked with aircraft systems.

I had offers from RCA in New Jersey, AT&T Labs, also in New Jersey, a government job in Mobile, Ala at Brookley AFB and Boeing in Seattle, Washington. Boeing offered me a job working on the BOMARC missile system and I took this for several reasons. The pay was almost the best, starting at $5,250 per year (1958 pay scale), fit into my dream of reaching into space and Seattle was the furthest away from New Orleans and rising interference from Shirley's family.

So we packed our "bags", the moving van came to pick up our furniture and off the three of us went in our Olds bound for Seattle at the far corner of Pacific Northwest and a new life in a place neither of us had ever been.

The Boeing missile job

On arrival in Seattle, we rented an apartment and I reported to work the following Monday. I was assigned to work on the final design of the BOMARC which became the first supersonic unmanned interceptor of unfriendly aircraft for the cold war North America Defense system (NORAD). The BOMARC also became the first long range anti aircraft missile. This assignment fit into my dream of reaching out into space but was cut short after just a few months.

When the moving van driver knocked on our apartment door to deliver all our things from Baton Rouge including the new furniture we had just bought in a great sale(Boeing paid for the moving), he said "Did you know the truck had an accident just outside Seattle and that your furniture was severely damaged? But not to worry, Boeing is responsible for repairing or replacing everything. As the furniture was brought into the apt., we saw it was basically in pieces.

When days grew into weeks and into three months and nothing was done except an offer to glue the pieces together which to us was unacceptable, I took out the letter my college professor had given me introducing me to one of the Boeing vice presidents and went to see him. When he asked "Son, how is it all going?, I told him about the hassles we were having with the Boeing insurance department. The next day on getting to work, I was called into the personnel dept and warned 'How dare you seeing a vice president without approval of your supervisor?" I was warned that if I didn't promptly accept whatever was offered by the Boeing insurance department and promising to correct my ways, my career at Boeing would not be helped.

Luckily I still had the Bell Labs offer and when I called that day to check to see if it still was open and heard "yes" with the added comment "When are you coming?", I replied that I was also still available and accepted the offer. When getting home from work that day, I told Shirley to start packing because I had just accepted the Bell Labs job and was waiting for the written offer.

The following morning, I handed my two week notice resigning my job at Boeing citing the reason. But when receiving the telegram from AT& T the very next day we were surprised to learn that instead of moving to New Jersey and the Labs, I would be assigned as a field engineer to the U.S. Marine Corps base at 29 Palms, Calif. to train the Marines in the use of the new surface to air Terrier Missile. However, I would first have to report to the Field Engineering head office at Winston Salem, NC for indoctrination. I left Shirley for one week flying to North Carolina and then back when we packed and left Seattle driving down to 29 Palms which was in the Mojave Desert about 150 miles east of Los Angeles.

Marine Corps Desert Training Twentynine Palms, Calif. 1958-1959

Twentynine Palms is on the Mojave Desert about 150 miles east of Los Angeles. Mojave Desert is also known as the 'high desert" because it lies on a 2000 ft. high plateau of mostly barren mountains with vast stretches of sand and rock. To the south is the Joshua Tree National Monument, A National park of giant cactus trees. Just to the south is a 3,000 ft. drop down to the Colorado Desert and Palm Springs.

To the north is famed Air Force Edwards AFB famed for being the place where Col Chuck Yaeger and Scott Crossfield flew the X-15 manned rockets becoming the first astronauts(flying weightless above 100,000 ft). In a later chapter, I mention working personally with Scott Crossfield then a vice president at Eastern Airlines).

To the west lies the famed San Andreas Fault where far below lies the seismic plates causing much of the areas earthquakes. Although people didn't have to worry about hurricanes, there were sand storms you wanted to avoid because if you got caught in one while driving, your car paint would be stripped like in a sand blast and the windshield pitted. One good thing about being on the high desert was looking at the stars and planets with my new telescope because the high altitude air was bluer with the images clearer due to the extremely low moisture.

Twentynine Palms then was a small place in the middle of the desert serving the Marine Corps base with scattered trailers and remote homes of hermits and retirees. It had one drug store, one food store, a hardware store, and a post office and residential areas where Marine Corps personnel lived. The town plumber was the brother of actress Esther Williams, famed for swimming clothes modeling and movies.

We rented a two bedroom house at the edge of town which actually was just one block from the center. Thankfully, it was air conditioned which in the desert is critical as temps can rise to 120 degrees in the summer heat.

But the desert air conditioner is not what you may be familiar with. It is a cooling tower sitting on the roof where air is blown through a wall of falling water which is cooled by a refrigeration coil. When the air is passed through the cooled water, it becomes humidified and cooled before going into the house via ducts. This is the opposite of a regular air conditioner where humidity is extracted from the air. There was a small yard at the front of the house with sand, rock and a few cactuses.

I reported in at the company field office lead by the supervisor, Bill Withers and one other, Wilmer Price. The three of us would work out of an office on base and go on field training missions.

The work consisted refining with operations and maintenance manuals for the Terrier surface to air missile and teaching the Marines in its use. We went on many field desert operations with actual Marine units. This Marine Corps base is still where Marines are sent for desert operations training which became especially useful during the Mideast operations in Iraq and Afghanistan.

We encountered two major problems at 29 Palms. We found only one other Jewish person there and she apparently moved to 29 Palms to get away from the Jews. So here we were trying to be allowed to use the officers club and later learned why we had a problem being admitted. This lady did her best to keep us out.

The other problem was that the pharmacist of the only drugstore in town was Catholic who refused to carry contraceptives forcing us to shop in the nearest larger town which was Riverside. But to get to Riverside we had to drive through a winding mountain road down Gorgonio Pass and Shirley often got car sick. Why was the pharmacy a problem? One time, Shirley had run out of "supplies" and whammo,, she got pregnant.

Bye Bye California
New Jersey, here we come

One day coming home from work in the spring 1959, I surprisingly heard Shirley talking to someone and wondered who was visiting when we really had no friends in this lonely desert town. When I saw her talking to the sofa and somehow it seemed to answer, I knew it was time to leave 29 Palms and get back to civilization. I sent a message to my supervisor telling him that nine months in the desert was long enough and it was time to leave. I either would get transferred to the Bell Labs in New Jersey where I was supposed to be in the first place or I would find a new job.

We lucked out. It took only two days to get an answer. We were being transferred to Whippany, NJ. which is Bell Labs military development lab. We packed and the company arranged for the moving company to do the rest. Since Shirley was pregnant and got car sick easily, the company agreed to include her going by air via a stop in New Orleans to stay with her parents while I drove the 3000 miles across the country and when I got to NJ, she would be flown there from New Orleans. We even were given relocation benefits including six months rent and furniture storage until we were permanently settled. That was how engineers were treated in those days.

After the moving van left and we had our car packed along with our year old son, I drove us all to the Los Angeles airport and put them on a DC 7 (propeller aircraft) and said "See you all in New Jersey". Wait for my call.

The Interstate expressways hadn't arrived yet so after dropping Shirley off at the LAX airport, I headed east on Route 66 all the way to Chicago. This route would take me right past the Meteor Crater near Flagstaff in northern Arizona. I stopped there to see the crater, again fulfilling my deep interest in things about space and the unknown. I arrived to Whippany, NJ five days later reporting to my new job.

Bell Labs, the holy grail

On arriving, I learned that I was offered temp living assistance for six months as part of my transfer benefits which included an apartment in Newark and furniture storage until we found permanent housing. I accepted the Ivy Hill apartments in Newark which was next to a nice park. Shirley could walk to and immediately made arrangements for Shirley and the baby to fly to New Jersey, our new home.

The relocation office gave me a list of rentals and houses to buy. I found a place called Birchwood Village on a hill overlooking Dover, a city just 15 minutes from work where new houses were being built. As soon as Shirley arrived, I took her to see this place and we bought our first house, a 3 bedroom two bath split level with a garage, basement and rec room with a great view of the city below and hills beyond. It was a nothing down, VA loan and would be ready in 6 months.

The job took me down to earth from the missile work done in Seattle and California. I was assigned to the "Cryogenics Lab" where was being developed a super high speed magnetic storage system for super computers. The theory was that super high computer speeds were possible if the data would be stored magnetically at extreme low temperatures all the way down to "Absolute Zero" which is minus 459 degrees F and called Zero on the Kelvin scale.

Our life in Dover, NJ

Our new son, Kenneth, was born June 29, 1959 at East Orange, NJ hospital while we still lived in the Ivy Hill apartments. Shirley's mother came to help for a week. Unfortunately, Shirley lost her Mom shortly thereafter. She worked hard all her life and I believe her passing away at a young age of about 57 was simply being worn out,

I converted a regular stroller into a double stroller so Shirley could take both boys, only 15 months apart in age, to the park. Some people thought they were twins.

When the house in Dover was ready, we moved in and Shirley started meeting nice neighbors. There were many employees living in the area whose husbands worked at nearby Picatinny Arsenal which was the Army base developing armaments and Rocketdyne where solid motors for space rockets were developed and tested.. We lived in this house five years until 1964 when we moved to Cape Canaveral, Florida, America's gateway to space.

Winters were brutal. One day, during a snow storm, it took me 6 hours to drive from work and had to leave the car at the bottom of the hill leading to our house because it was sliding back down as I tried to drive up. That became a deciding factor when the offer came to move to Cape Canaveral, Florida.

The weather caused me bad sinus problems but I was lucky meeting Dr. Rubens, the local ENT doctor. He had developed an effective remedy for my problem. Taking a pipe cleaner dipped in a solution of iodine and jamming it up my nose all the way into the upper sinus cavity. It was a crude fix but worked. It cleared my sinuses without a doubt and I'll never forget that pipe cleaner nor Dr. Rubens.

During summers we took the kids to Wildwood on the South Jersey shore where we flew kites on the beach. Occasionally, we drove to see uncle Alfred and aunt Elsie on the chicken farm in south Jersey.

Gunther Karger

Our favorite dinner place was the 'Three Sisters" on route 46 in Rockaway where we always had its famous Roast Duck.

Our First house

Our sons, Herbert & Kenneth

Gunther & the IEEE

Bell Labs encouraged all its scientists and engineers to join technical societies to learn the latest innovations in technology. Since I was already a member of the IRE(Institute of Radio Engineers) having joined it as a student member at LSU. I went to the first monthly meeting I could. This would change my life because at the IRE meetings I met the leaders of that day in electronics. I met George Anderson, president of Edison Labs. Edison Labs created by Thomas Edison was still inventing things at its East Orange lab. There was Allen Dumont, the inventor of color TV and founder of the Dumont TV Network, Allen Parks, president of Boonton Electric and a pioneer in electronic measurements and Chuck Vadersen, a leader at ITT labs pioneering air navigation systems. I was in awe meeting George Bailey, the founder of amateur radio which made possible for people to communicate with each other all over the world using home based radio transmitters.

These two societies merged in 1964 to become the IEEE (Institute of Electrical and Electronics Engineers) of which I became a charter member since I was a member of both IRE and AIEE at that time.

Northern New Jersey during my time was what Silicon Valley in California became later on. In fact it was the three scientists from Bell Labs who invented the transistor who moved to California creating what the micro chip and related industries have become today. At the encouragement and support of Bell Labs, I became involved actively with these historic technology leaders including John Pierce who is considered "Father of Satellite Communications".

Shirley almost always came with me to our monthly meetings because these were dinner meetings attended by members and many wives. Although these were pioneering technical development times, it also became socially involved as many of us developed friendships lasting years. She eventually evolved into being hostess to many meetings and conventions.

Eventually, I was elected to the position of Chairman of the IEEE Communications Group (later known as "Society") and as such became leader of the largest professional society of technical communications in the birthplace of modern communications and the youngest ever to reach such position. This was already reaching far above the 13 year old war orphan arriving to the U.S alone and with nothing.

Gunther–the Satellite Engineer

Although I completed my engineering assignments in cryogenic magnetic computer storage research, I became more and more involved with the IEEE and was eventually appointed to the IEEE Northern New Jersey Executive Board responsible for coordinating its various professional groups representing technical specialties. These included Satellites, military communications, power engineering, networks, vehicular communications and others numbering about a dozen. When somehow it was discovered that I had a writing talent, I was appointed to write about these things including technical developments.

These activities led me to meet industry and technical leaders and eventually to a job offer from ITT (International Telephone and Telegraph Laboratories) in Nutley to work on developing Courier Satellite which would be the world's first active communication satellite. Although it would mean leaving Bell Labs and facing a daily commute of about 30 miles to Nutley which was not far from the Lincoln tunnel to New York city, the opportunity and challenge to again join the exploration into space and the dream I had in Sweden years before outweighed the commute. Shirley agreed and became the wife of a commuter who left for work when it was dark and came back often after dark.

I was assigned the job of designing the up/down telemetry link to the satellite and participated in the project through its launch at Cape Canaveral late 1960. There was an article in the Dover Times listing "Gunther Karger as one of three engineers who developed the Courier Satellite". I had "arrived" to the world of space I dreamed of many years before reading comic strips about Buck Rogers.

Microwave Services calls

One day, I received a call from Victor Nexon, the president of MSI (Microwave Services International) inviting me to join a new team to design the first transcontinental microwave system from the East coast to California as consultant to Western Union which would operate the system. This would be the backbone transmission system over which telephone, data, video and all the primary communication traffic would flow. My job would be to decide where the microwave towers would be placed as this was a line of sight system requiring towers about every 25 miles.

This offer came at a good time because the Courier satellite project was near completion and I would be reassigned to some other yet unknown project. Another benefit would be that the head MSI office was located in Denville, NJ only 10 minutes from our house.

My job would be to analyze special aerial photographs called photogrammetry contour maps giving elevations using 3D cameras and from these, I would decide exactly where the towers would be placed subject to some field inspections. This led to some field trips into the wilderness including specifically Shadow Mountain just south of Bakersfield, California. I had rented a car and drove to this site not realizing I would be going to a rattle snake infested rocky mountain which no one should be going to alone. I learned about radio propagation principles including the importance of refraction of the microwave beam due to atmospheric conditions such as salt content of air in a path crossing Salt Lake in Utah.

On this assignment I met Fred Westheimer, the project's chief engineer and his wife, Ruth Westheimer who later would become "Dr. Ruth" of TV fame. More about them in a later chapter.

The Venezuela Electric Project

As my assignment on the Western union project neared completion, Victor assigned me the task of preparing a study for modernizing the electric company of Caracas, Venezuela. The purpose of this was to help the electric company get a $50 million loan from the World Bank.

This project would become the one on which I would become expert in effective report writing making complex things simple for non technical financial people. I learned all about an electric company, its communications and control systems and the relationship between operating requirements and project funding. This would become my "Doctorate Thesis" in consulting and technical presentations. What I learned from Victor on this project became invaluable for the rest of my life. I did the entire project from start to finish under Victor's personal guidance and the electric utility did get the $50 million for its modernization.

The Bulova Caper

One day, I received a phone call from a member of the board of the Bulova Corporation which had grown into a multi billion dollar conglomerate far more than a watch company. He wanted us to evaluate a potential acquisition and investigate the acquisition candidate. I told my boss, Victor (the company president) and said I am not qualified to do a mergers and acquisition project. What should I tell the Bulova guy? Victor said call back and accept the job and that I would be doing it. He had learned that I was very diverse and could do almost anything.

So, I accepted the assignment and investigated the potential acquisition which was a small marine electronics company making ship to shore radios and related marine electronic systems. The first problem I encountered was that I couldn't find any Hartman Marine products on the market nor any readily available financial information about the company. So I drove to the company's address in Long Island and did find the company. But it was nothing more than a second floor loft warehouse with some old radio equipment and no employees. It seemed to be a dead company.

I put my new investigators hat on and dug deeper to find out who really owned this so called company and why would a prime time corporation want to buy it? I found the answer! The owner was a cousin of the Bulova board director who had made a deal of selling it to Bulova for a tidy sum with a commission to be paid to the Bulova relative. This guy had called my company in the belief that we wouldn't know better and just "bless" the deal to earn a consulting fee. But what he didn't know was that it was me, Gunther Karger, he called and that I then was and remain today a person of high ethical values who can smell a rat.

The report I wrote was not the one the Bulova guy wanted nor expected. I stated that Hartman Marine Electronics was a worthless shell company and recommended that Bulova would not acquire it. The call I received form the Bulova director was one I likely won't ever forget. After chewing my ass out, he fired me.

I told Victor who had approved my report, But he said that I better do whatever it would take to get paid or he would withhold my paycheck. We had done a professional job, had earned our fee and would be paid. How was up to me.

I simply sent a bill for our services to the Bulova CEO attaching the report I had written with a cover note about how we were given the assignment and the threat by one of his board members. In my cover note I clearly stated that unless we received full payment for our services within 30 days, I would turn the file over to the U.S. attorney charging fraud involving a public corporation.

We received our full payment within one week with a special thanks and we noted in the news that the Bulova director had resigned.

I didn't know it then, but that would be my introduction to corporate fraud investigations which eventually led me to a new career after my adventures into space ended.

When money speaks, truth keeps silent
Russian Proverb

The Cold War Calls

It was about 1962 with the Cold War in full swing. The news focused on the U.S. and Soviet Union targeting nuclear armed ICBM's (Intercontinental Ballistic Missiles) against each other and the public was encouraged to make personal emergency plans in case of a nuclear attack.

I had continued my work in the IEEE and my professional achievements became recognized more and more. One of the persons on my communications group committee was Roger Mc Sweeney who recently retired as Chief Engineer at RCA Communications. He asked me to have lunch and offered me an opportunity with a new company being formed of which he was a Director.

The company would be known as ITT Communication Systems (ICS) to be constituted by three leading companies in the defense communications industry which were ITT Laboratories, RCA, Hughes Electronics and Hoffman Electronics with most personnel contributed from those companies. I had been nominated as part of the ITT contingent since I had worked for ITT Labs and was proposed to serve as Project Manager of Strategic Command Control Communications Systems.

My responsibility would be to develop a system providing the general in the Airborne Command Post operating 24/7 the capability to deploy an emergency communication system for the USA that would survive an attack by 100 nuclear bombs destroying most major cities and military bases. This special system also would be capable of providing the communications enabling the general to deploy a lethal retaliatory attack against the Soviet Union using the North Atlantic Submarine Fleet.

The operation would be headed by Lt. General Roy Lynn from the NSA (National Security agency) and my direct boss would be Dr. R.R. Rooney who had just retired from the CIA as Associate Director of Communications. The company would report to the office of Secretary of Defense and work with a White House coordinator. I also would work with an Air Force supervisor at the Air Force Systems Command with HQ at Hanscom field near Boston. The office for the group of about 100 people would be in Paramus in a highly secure building.

This sounded like a "Jack Ryan" tale right out of Tom Clancy's books and an adventure not to have been even dreamt of by a war refugee with aspirations of exploring space. I would have access to defense contractors including famed Booz Allen Hamilton (McLean, Virginia), MITRE (MIT Research & Engineering) in Lexington, Mass. and work directly with top Air Force generals at the Pentagon and SAC HQ in Omaha, Neb.

I said "YES" and agreed to report after the two week notice I would give Victor Nexon and his MSI. I told Shirley of this new adventure but that we wouldn't need to move as I could commute from our Dover house to Paramus. There also would be frequent travel to the Pentagon in Washington, Boston (MIT) and Omaha, Nebraska where Hq. Strategic Air Command is located at Offutt AFB as well as California visiting major aerospace companies to evaluate their technologies. This was a dream job working with the top leaders in technology and national security.

The ICS Doomsday Group

ICS was basically constituted as a "think tank" assigned the task of developing and implementing a system needed for survival if the Russians managed to launch 100 nuclear bombs against the USA. This group was unlike any other that ever had been created. It was concerned about dealing with potential threats which had never before been experienced and hoped never would materialize. It was this group that became part of the policy of 'Deterrence" which ruled and eventually won the Cold War.

This was making sure the "enemy" would know that that if they launched a first strike of nuclear missiles, they would suffer consequence potentially capable of destroying not only themselves, but the world. It is believed that this is what caused the Russians to stand down in the Cuban missile crisis and led to the creation of the "Hotline" between the White House and Kremlin as a last means of taking a "breather" before either side would risk "pressing the nuclear button".

We developed and implemented among other things the "SIOP" (Single Integrated Operations Plan) for the doomsday scenario making the U.S. ready for immediate reaction and be much better prepared for a major nuclear attack far greater than Hiroshima and Nagasaki.

Unfortunately, the ICS group was dissolved after it had completed its task. Had it been continued in some form after the Cold War, it likely would have prevented the 9/11 disaster. I confirmed this speaking with the Executive Director of the 9/11 Commission at a meeting on "Terrorism for the 21st Century" to which I had been invited and held in 2006.

Most of the ISC staff members were very senior people from whom I learned a great deal. I was probably the youngest on the team working routinely with top generals and very senior industry & government officials. Below are of pictures of our ICS Group and two generals I personally worked with.

Gen. Lynn (NSA) and the ICS staff.
Gunther with glasses

Maj. Gen. John Bestic   Maj. Gen. Gordon Gould
Commander Air Force SystemsStrategic Command

AFSACS

While at ICS, I was assigned two basic tasks. The first was to provide the general in the airborne command post the capability to send command signals to the North Atlantic submarine fleet with orders to launch a retaliatory attack after 100 nuclear bombs exploded in the U.S. destroying most communications with the bomb's EMP(electro magnetic pulse). I overcame this problem by designing a deep underground facility capable of launching an electric helicopter driven by a power cable which also served as the 1000 ft ELF antenna. ELF(Extra Low Frequency) has the capability of reaching global distances and also penetrating the ocean surface so the subs could receive the signal. Although this system was approved for development, it was never implemented because some believed it was too much "science fiction".

The second task was to provide an emergency backup communications capability for essential communications covering most of the U.S. This took the form of C-130 aircraft operating at 30,000 ft as transponders and a digital address system using advanced signaling techniques. I called this "AFSACS" standing for Air Force Survivable Airborne Communication System which in effect would have been the first cellular communication system twenty years ahead of the commonly known debut of cell telephone in the mid 80's.

I personally developed the briefings for these systems and presented them to top Pentagon offices.

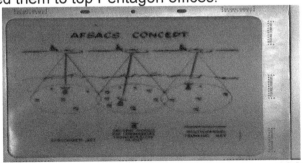

The original chart I presented Pentagon, 1963

Editor of the International IEEE Communications Society Newsletter

I will forever be grateful to Ransom Slayton, the chairman of the IEEE Communications Society who asked me to serve as Editor of its monthly newsletter circulated worldwide to over 35,000 members. Ransom lived in Chicago, worked at Teletype Corp. (an AT & T Company) and was the inventor of the teletype machine. Shirley & I visited him several times at his home in Skokie and we kept in touch until he passed away years later.

The IEEE Communications Newsletter had been published for many years when I took it over from Ray Bogdan, its previous Editor. I was assisted by two associate editors one on the West coast and the other in Chicago while I also served the east coast. The publication under my six year tenure grew to nearly 50 pages and was in fact a "magazine". It was my job to get the news of society activities and members worldwide and put it together. This was before the time of personal computers and word processors so I had to use a typewriter and pasted & clipped it together. Then I sent it to the IEEE Hq. in New York for the actual printing and distribution.

This experience was one of the most significant of my career because added to my capability of gathering information and working with people all of whom, including myself, were unpaid volunteers. We all believed in the importance of furthering communications technology and the interests of the engineers who were creating an industry which eventually transformed the world.

What you see today in globalized e-commerce and personal communications from anywhere to anywhere at anytime whether in office, home, or on the move was basically created during this time. This is the indirect benefit of the Moon Program of the sixties and the Cold War.

The Westheimer Episode

I had mentioned in the Microwave Services (MSI) chapter that I worked with its Chief Engineer, Fred Westheimer. We established a friendship lasting for many years because we had in common both of us and his wife, Ruth, being Holocaust survivors originally from Germany. Ruth at that time was a graduate student at Columbia University getting her PhD in Psychology.

When I left MSI for ICS to my Cold War assignment, I arranged for Fred to get an offer also which he accepted and thus, he joined ICS. The work we all did was very sensitive requiring the highest national security clearance level. When I learned that Fred's wife, Ruth was involved with a communist cell at Columbia University, I had the unpleasant task to tell Fred that his wife had 24 hours to dissociate herself from that group or face losing the job he just got.

Fortunately for all, that all worked out and eventually, Fred's wife became the famous TV sex doctor "Dr. Ruth". Unfortunately, Fred had a skiing accident leading to him eventually suffering a fatal fall down the steps in his NYC apt.

While Fred & I worked at ICS and I served as Chairman of the IEEE Communication Group, I had appointed him to be "Facilities Chairman" responsible for making sure everything was in order for our meetings such as the room, projectors etc. We had a meeting scheduled in the basement auditorium of the Garden State Plaza across the street from our office. Gen. John Bestic, then the Air Force Chief of Command Control in the Pentagon was our guest speaker.

After our usual pre-meeting dinner at which Shirley was our official hostess, we all went downstairs to the auditorium. I introduced the general and then suddenly, frost instead of heat came out of the air conditioning ducts. I asked Fred to go in the back room to check the controls and when he did, the lights went out and everybody left since it got freezing cold in this January New Jersey evening.

A month later while attending a meeting at the Pentagon in Washington, as I rounded a corner, I saw Gen . Bestic and I quickly made an about face to avoid him. I'll never forget him yelling out "Gunther, did you bring the blanket?". Gen. Bestic by then had been elevated to Air Force Chief of Staff.

I thought it would add flavor to "My Story" to include "The **Westheimer** Episode". Although Fred died years ago, "Dr. Ruth" still appears on TV and gives speeches. But she still hates me for the incident at Columbia University.

Roger Mc Sweeney

I would be remiss not including the person I respected the most and who probably was responsible for the opportunity I was given working on the ISC team.

Roger Mc Sweeney had just retired as Chief Engineer at RCA Communications International at its HQ in NYC. Roger was responsible for installing telephone systems throughout Latin America including Cuba. I found few people knowing more about communications than Roger and learned a great deal from him. Shirley & I became close friends with Roger and his wife, Ruth and kept up after the ICS team disbanded. I often had dinner with them on some of my trips to Washington where they moved from New Jersey after ICS ended. Roger was a person to be remembered and as he and Ruth had no children, I want to "remember" Roger Mc Sweeney in this book.

Florida Calls
Fall 1964

What does one do when the New Jersey winter approaches and sunny calls with a job offer?

The ICS mission was nearing completion and the company was being sold to Computer Sciences corp. (CSC) with the office being relocated to CSC's Hq in Washington. I also was conditionally offered a position in the White House "Office of Telecommunications Policy" to be headed by Chuck Lathey whose appointment to "Director of telecommunications Policy was pending.

We decided to accept the offer from the "Sun" which was as Associate Principal Engineer at Radiation Inc, Melbourne, FL which is just south of Cape Canaveral and Cocoa Beach. The job would be to develop advanced military communication systems. All moving expenses would be paid, I would get a raise and avoid the winter just ahead. However, I did keep the White House option open just in case it did "come in" even after we moved to Florida.

And so, we packed our bags, the moving van came and we left our Dover house and New Jersey in the new 1964 Dodge Dart we had just bought. The "dream" I had long ago in Sweden from reading Buck Rogers stories was getting closer to reality. We were moving to "Moon Port USA" where the rockets were going up now on a routine basis. I was familiar with the area having been there on trips in connection with the courier Satellite launches.

Satellite Beach
where we watched the rockets

Satellite Beach, Florida is a residential town about 10 miles south of Cape Canaveral which was considered Moonport USA in the 1960's. We immediately bought a new house, the second house we would own. It was a 3/2 with a two car garage, enclosed patio pool, only a few blocks from the Atlantic Ocean beach and only 20 minutes from work.

We bought the boys each a surfboard so they could walk to the beach and surf. In the picture at right, our sons, Herb & Ken are selling lemonade from our front yard. They got to school on their bicycles.

Shirley made good friends quickly as she always did. It wasn't long before my phone rang from the local IEEE chapter president. Word had gotten to Cape Canaveral that "Gunther Karger, the IEEE leader had moved there from New Jersey and invited me to the next meeting. It wasn't long before I was invited to its executive board, elected as secretary, then vice chairman and in 1968, I was elected Chairman of the largest chapter in the world with membership of about 3000.

Gunther at Cape Canaveral

The job at Radiation Inc (later became Harris Corp) didn't work out well. It became clear after just a few months that I was hired mostly for "who I knew" rather than for "what I knew" as my assignments tapered off as soon as I had introduced the big bosses to my high level Washington and industry contacts, This led me to accept an offer I also had from Pan Am Aerospace at Cocoa Beach in its communications planning dept. where I got a standing assignment to make sure there were the proper communications in place for space and missile launches. But I learned early on that the head of this group was a retired Air Force Colonel who spent more time at a bar than in the office and a civilian supervisor who was way past his retirement age.

A high level civil service position opened at the John F. Kennedy Space Center(at Cape Canaveral also) and I was invited to apply. I passed all the qualifications and was about to be offered the position when another retired colonel shows up getting the job.

All this added to the growing political pressures to reduce aerospace costs became signs that it may be time to evaluate my career direction. I started to look at other industries needing my "expertise" which was innovation and led me to the airline industry which at that time had engineering departments looking like situations needing refurbishment.

The Nazis found me in Florida

I had become friends with a Cliff Mattox who sort of was a "Senior Statesman" to the engineers at Cape Canaveral. Cliff was on the U.S. intelligence team sent to Germany right after its WW II surrender to "retrieve" Hitler's rocket team before the Russians got to them. Cliff and his team managed to get most of them including Dr. Vernher von Braun, the famed rocket engineer responsible for the V1 and V2 rockets that pelted London. Cliff told me many stories about this.

The German rocket team still led by von Braun had been taken to a U.S. Army camp in New Mexico for indoctrination into American life and further assignments in military rocket engineering. One day when the team was gathered waiting for a meeting to start, von Braun entered the room as all rose with the outstretched "Heil Hitler" salute. According to Cliff, this indicated that further deprogramming was needed. Apparently the deprogramming given in New Mexico wasn't enough and showed up when I was nominated to become the next IEEE chairman at Cape Canaveral.

The Cape Canaveral area inclusive of Cocoa Beach, Melbourne, Satellite Beach was also the new home of former German rocket scientists who now had top jobs in the space industry. One of them was Dr. Horst who also was on the IEEE executive committee serving as treasurer. He was one of those people who thrived on titles(as most nobility does) while leaving the work to others.

So when the IEEE board nominated me to become its next Chairman, there was objection from Dr. Horst. He had been there before me and was far more a senior person job wise. He believed he was way ahead of me (especially since he learned I was not only Jewish, but a Jewish refugee from the Holocaust created by the Nazis).

The Executive Committee consisting of Chairman, Vice Chairman, Secretary and treasurer is elected by is membership in an actual election subject to the nomination of the nominating committee. When the nominating committee asked me to run for the election, I accepted on the condition that the then current treasurer would not be nominated to serve on my team and only because he never did any work such as writing checks and keeping the books. This infuriated Dr. Horst who filed for his own election by petition which was duly circulated in the IEEE local newsletter,.

But, that wasn't enough for Dr. Horst. Since there were 3000 members living in the area, Dr. Horst started to go door to door soliciting support for his own election. This was a most unusual thing for professionals to do, One day, when I opened the Cocoa Beach Edition of the Orlando Sentinel paper what did I see as the top front page headline? "Engineers run agog over its election of chairman". I promptly informed the nominating committee that I would withdraw from the race because I would not be involved with such unprofessional actions. The committee refused my withdrawal and I was elected.

This to me was extraordinarily important because the Nazis killed my family in Germany but here in the U.S. I beat one of them in an election.

But did I really win? A month later my boss calls me in to his office and lays me off citing budget reductions and job eliminations. The Space race to Moon was already fading with Cape Canaveral full of no longer necessary engineers, myself being one. It didn't seem to matter that just two weeks after being elected Chairman, I also had received an award as 'Outstanding Man of America". Dr. Horst prevailed as did all of his former German team members kept their jobs but I lost mine. Was the hand of the past somewhere in all this?

I then realized that the Space Program no longer was the frontier it had been as it became invaded by bureaucrats while the federal budget was being reduced. It was time to "move on" to find a new challenge.

Outstanding Man of America Award(1967)

Although no longer living in New Jersey, I continued on several national industry committees including serving as Editor of the IEEE Communications Group Newsletter which had a worldwide circulation of about 35,000. My appointment to the IEEE Russian Technology Assessment committee and continued leadership in the technical world of communications in addition to my role in preventing a nuclear war (my work at ICS) led to my nomination and award as "Outstanding young Man of America" by International Jaycees (Junior Chamber of Commerce International) in 1967. Being elected youngest ever Chapter Chairman of the IEEE at Cape Canaveral was also a significant factor leading to this unusual recognition of an immigrant who came to America alone as a war orphan at age 13.

I was given a gold tie pin which I proudly continue wearing on my ties as I also at the same time to this day wear the "Gripsholm" pin I bought while aboard the Gripsholm when coming to America in 1946. Receiving many awards and token of recognition, this designation to me represents the highest achievement an immigrant and war orphan could receive.

The 1966 Space Congress
Cocoa Beach Hilton

During the heady days of America's Moon program, Cape Canaveral became the "Mecca" of the space industry. This is where "It happened" and all those who counted would eventually gather at some launch, industry event or live there as we did. Cape Canaveral became America's gateway to space.

A favorite watering hole became The Polaris Motel" on the beach in Cocoa Beach which was the city just south of the Air Force launch facility called Cape Canaveral and later the John F. Kennedy Space Center operated by NASA . Over time, hotels and many restaurants sprang up including the Cocoa Beach Hilton where we had many meetings both local and national.

One such event was the International Space Congress which was for a time held annually. While serving as chairman of the Canaveral IEEE chapter and still Editor of the IEEE international Communications Newsletter, I served on the Space Congress committee in 1966. The keynote speaker would be Vice President Hubert Humphries who also was then the chairman of the National Aeronautics and Space Council. The sponsor of the event was Canaveral society of Technical Societies of which I was a board member since I was chairman of one of its key member organizations.

For Shirley, this would become an important event also because she was the official hostess to the event's banquet at which the Vice President spoke and she was the person who officially greeted the Vice President. Over the years, Shirley had became the official hostess at IEEE events where I officiated. She became the "First Lady" of the IEEE at Cape Canaveral during America's Moon program. She was in her glory at that event.

That was a day to be remembered as part of the decade when Cape Canaveral became the pride of America.

Our world travels with Pan Am

The Pan Am job had a great extra benefit. Although I worked for Pan Am's Aerospace Services Division, I was still eligible for company's worldwide space available almost free air travel on Pan Am flights.

The first trip we took was to Europe in summer, 1966 for our two week vacation. We made arrangements for our two sons to go to a YMCA summer camp at Camp Winona in Central Florida. Then we flew to Stockholm and took the train to Stora Skedvi in Dalarna to visit the Gustafssons and all the people in that Swedish village who kept me after fleeing Germany in 1939.

This was for us a historic visit starting with our arrival at the train station. Nearly the entire village was waiting for us as the train arrived with everyone waving hello. This was the first time we had seen them since I was packed off in 1944 to be sent to the Jewish orphanage. We would visit them and the village many times during our 20 years with Eastern Airlines because working for Eastern, I also had standby near free flying benefits. We sent our sons several times to be on their farm during summer vacations so our sons could get some understanding not only about the world, but of their heritage.

We had planned to go to Barcelona, Spain for the second week of this first trip to Europe. So we got on a plane in Stockholm bound for London where we were to change planes for Barcelona. However, we were told all connecting flights were booked for several days. So we asked if there were flights available for other destinations not mattering where so long as it would not be back to the U.S.. Yes, Pan Am's round the world flight would leave 7:00 am with first stop in Frankfurt going on to Istanbul, Karachi and onward. I tell the agent to put us on it…we'll fly round the world for our second week of our vacation instead of Spain. So we got a blanket, found a bench and slept in the airport until the flight left early morning.

After being awakened early in the morning for breakfast, there was a big commotion among the passengers. Since this flight was going to Turkey and Pakistan where most people are Muslim, lots of passengers were Muslim. When the breakfast was served with ham, the Muslims nearly rioted because they can't eat ham. Then, the flight attendant came to us telling us we had to deplane in Frankfurt because we had to have visas for Pakistan and had to get off.

So now we were stranded in Frankfurt. What would we do? We rented a car and drove south toward Switzerland. I then realized that we would be passing near my German hometown. So we got off the autobahn and actually drove to Schmieheim looking for my house which we did find. But we just kept on driving through on to Switzerland where we spent a few days before getting a plane returning from Zurich.

The second and last trip was in 1967 just before the Pan Am job ended. While IEEE chairman at Cape Canaveral, I had made contact with the president of the IEEE president of Australia who invited us. Again, we sent the kids to the same summer camp and we left for two days in Hawaii, then off to Hong Kong for another two days before taking off on a nonstop to Sydney, Australia. On arrival early in the morning after flying all night, we saw a sign with our name. A committee of three people were meeting us at the airport including the Australian IEEE president. One of these was Bryan Nolte, the head of the Philips Australia company who took us to the best downtown hotel and hosted us for nearly a week. We became lifetime friends with us visiting the Nolte's Cambridge(UK) and Singapore on later trips. The Nolte's even visited us in Miami on their way moving back home to Australia from Cambridge.

Years later while working at Eastern Airlines, we flew to Australia three times to see the Nolte's and much of Australia including once to the Great Barrier Reef. The Nolte's are both "gone" but we maintain occasional contact with their son David and daughter, Anne Marie.

The end at Cape Canaveral arrived

Shortly after being given my Pan Am layoff notice, my phone rang. It was someone from Boeing offering me a job paying the same I was at the Pan Am job. Although the job was far remote from anything I had ever done, it was a job which put bread on the table and paid the mortgage payment. I took it because it gave me time to follow up on feelers I had already put out.

The Boeing job was on the NASA crawler tractor which is the huge structure on which the large moon type rockets are transported on rail from the VAB (Vehicle Assembly Building) to the launching pad). It was my job, along with at least 100 others to determine which parts of this humongous tractor would be damaged during blastoff.

Knowing this job would end as soon as the last Moon shot went off, I accelerated my looking for a new and challenging opportunity focusing on the airline industry.

Three months on the Boeing job, I received an offer from Eastern Airlines to come and restructure the Engineering Department. The job was at Eastern's Miami office and we would have to move to Miami. Concurrently, I also about the same time received the long awaited offer for the White House job. We had a family meeting to discuss whether to go back up north to the snow and cold or south to more sun and fishing.

The sun won and we headed south to Miami and yet another new career. What we didn't then know was that we would also go to a new world and an entirely different life never to return to aerospace.

Gunther Karger

Hello Miami and Eastern Airlines

The four of us arrived to Miami late fall, 1967 and checked into the Airport Holiday Inn where Eastern Airlines had booked us as part of the relocation deal. After reporting to the new job, we went house hunting and found our new home in an old avocado grove where a developer was selling lots and building houses in what seemed a jungle. Since the house wouldn't be ready for six months, the builder rented us a nearby house for almost nothing.

The home we built 1968 and lived 41 years until 2011
Set on a half acre in an avocado grove, four bedrooms, 2 baths, double garage, pool, Jacuzzi sauna and the jungle we created over the years. This is where we lived and raised our sons from age 10. It became known as the Jungle House .

Shirley and our Chrysler Sebring convertible

Gunther– the aircraft engineer

Although I was assigned to be the engineering supervisor of the Avionics Engineering Dept with specific responsibility for radars, navigations and communications, my primary focus was to bring the engineering dept. to the present "century". I had several old timers assigned to me who really resented someone coming in from the outside in a position higher than them. This became a challenge.

I really didn't know much about aircraft except flying in them so I decided to just dig in and learn all about aircraft engineering. So I showed up at the night shift in the maintenance hangar and just started working with the aircraft mechanics on the aircraft, in work clothes. How was I to change anything unless I knew what already was?

Over the following two years, I introduced new ways of doing things to improve aircraft avionic maintenance. For example, there was an above normal failure rate of the gyros, a critical navigation component and no one for several years could figure out the reason. Using a new failure analysis method I introduced, the real reason was identified. The gyro system uses a special gas bearing. The shop foreman had ordered replacement gas from a friend who sold cheaper gas, charged the company the current rate with the profits split between the foreman and the vendor. I replaced the vendor and use of the proper gas resolved the gyro failure rate. And, some heads gyrated out the door from the shop.

I often went on test flights(flying with no passengers). On one such test flight of a DC-9 aircraft on landing, the captain kept taxiing the aircraft right toward the firewall protecting the street beyond it outside the airport. I ordered the captain to relinquish controls to the co-pilot who immediately turned the aircraft away from the firewall. The captain was flying only to get flight premium pay. He was nearly blind in one eye. I saw to it that he was permanently grounded. He was the Airline's Chief Pilot.

Gunther - keynote speaker at Las Vegas convention

Word got out that I was someone more interested in the future than the present and was offered the job of "Project Engineer – New Aircraft". This assignment involved the evaluation of new aircraft and systems working closely with airplane companies like Boeing, Douglas and Lockheed.

This was also the time when the aviation industry was looking to develop VSTOL aircraft which could land on top of downtown "STOLPORTS" (very short runways) and even vertical takeoff/landings (not helicopters). I became the lead person to conduct this research & development project and was invited to speak at the annual Air Force Technology conference at the Sahara hotel in Las Vegas. There were three principal lunch speakers over the three day conference, Senator Barry Goldwater who was a presidential candidate, Gunther Karger (me) and Dr. Grover Loening with whom I had been working with on this project.

Dr. Loening was at the time in his 80's and the engineer who worked with the Wright Brothers designing the aircraft engines for the first flight at Kitty Hawk. He also was the person who set up the aircraft engine factory in Ohio, founded the Grumman Aircraft Corporation and designed the Loening amphibian airplane which became known as the "goose". Dr. Loening personally autographed his book "Takeoff into Greatness" which chronicles the birth of aviation with these words

*"**With my best regards to Gunther Karger, creator and builder of V-STOL aircraft, Grover Loening, Key Biscayne, Fl, Sept. 1970.**"* (see inscription inside book cover at right)

I always considered this a great honor especially for me, who came to this country as a 13 year old penniless war orphan and immigrant in 1946. It's noteworthy that Dr. Loening was also from Germany, as I was, born 1888 in Bremen, Germany.

Grover Loening, Left, and Orville Wright
...worked together at Wright plant in Dayton, Ohio

Dr. Grover Loeing with Orville Wright in 1913 and his personal handwritten note to Gunther in his book "Takeoff into Greatness" which is his book about the birth of aviation.

23 SEPT.

'GET ON WITH VTOL'
DR.GROVER LOENING

24 SEPT.

'COMMERCIAL V/STOL-
GOAL FOR 70'S'
GUNTHER KARGER

25 SEPT.

U.S.SENATOR
BARRY GOLDWATER

Gunther was luncheon keynote speaker at the Air Force Technology Conf. September 24, 1972 at the Sahara Hotel in Las Vegas along with Dr. Grover Loening, aviation pioneer and Sen/ Barry Goldwater, Presidential Candidate

Gunther and X-15
Rocket Pilot Scott Crossfield

My assignment at Eastern as Project Engineer led me to team up with Scott Crossfield who at the time was Eastern's Vice President of Flight Research & Development. Crossfield was the test pilot who along with Col. Chuck Yeager flew the X-15 rockets at Edwards AFB in the Calif. desert and was the first pilot designated as "Astronaut" qualifying for this distinction having flown above 100,000 ft. altitude.

Crossfield & I worked together on a number of aircraft projects focused on which type of aircaft Eastern should buy and the testing of them after major modifications.

Crossfield's career as test pilot unfortunately had ended when his rocket exploded on the launching pad injuring his eye sight. We often went to conferences together and one time at Houston, TX Space Flight meeting, he had me try out a real space suit. Crossfield, age 84, died in an airplane crash of a plane he piloted.

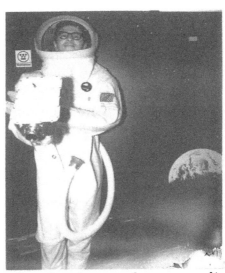

Gunther in a real space suit

Career change at age 40

Early 1972, I learned that Eastern wanted to start forecasting cargo revenue using computers, something that had never been done before. Word had somehow leaked to a top Eastern person that I was the person who developed the military intelligence communications system using a computer model designed by engineers at MITRE (MIT Research and Engineering Corp.).

The question came up if I might be interested in developing a cargo revenue forecasting system for Eastern Airlines. This was a substantial business segment with revenues of about $350 million annually. The assignment would also include the volume and revenue forecast for each station and there were about 125 of them throughout the U.S. and some international locations. The title offered at a paygrade increase was at the manager level and I would work in Eastern's corporate planning dept. which was about to move from the corporate HQ in NYC to Miami.

I had been getting a little bored anyway and even considered getting a job in Washington or California. We were settled in south Florida, the sun was shining instead of winter storms raging. I accepted the offer and that changed my career path forever. I didn't then know it but that took my primary work from technology to business.

This new job would last for 15 years until Eastern Airlines collapsed as a company and I retired not only from Eastern, but from permanent full time jobs.

Gunther the Airline forecaster

If something needs to be done and it never before has been done, give it to Gunther. He will find the way. That's the word that apparently preceded me getting this new assignment.

I had been promised help which did know something about computer programming and airline cargo but that hadn't arrived so I had to do this by myself.

Applying what I had learned in my military work days and Isaac Asimov's science fiction books, I used my newfound science of PHM (psycho Historic morphology) to get this job done. In six months, I had developed the Eastern Airline Cargo computerized forecasting and had it operating. I had created the capability of forecasting cargo traffic and revenue for the entire company not only for the total system, but for each of the 125 local stations round the world and track monthly how actuals performed vs the forecast. Importantly, I also had to get each manager responsible for creating and servicing this business to agree which meant I had to negotiate the forecast with about 50 people.

During the 15 years I was responsible for this task at Eastern Airlines, I was accurate to within 2% of the average $300 million annual revenue forecast which was unheard of in the industry. Over this 15 year time, I also became responsible for the company's economic planning and as such, influencing its total revenues which averaged $4 Billion annually.

Then I ran into the disaster which ultimately led to the destruction of Eastern Airlines which is covered in the following chapters.

The Bermuda Flight Bomb Threat

The flight had just departed from Bermuda for Baltimore with me aboard, having attended a meeting(1980) in Bermuda. About 45 minutes out of Bermuda, the captain announces" We have just received a bomb threat against this flight and are returning to Bermuda. Please fasten your seat belts and note that we are descending to a low altitude flight plan for your safety.

The plane dropped rapidly from about 35,000 ft. cruise altitude to about 500 ft. barely skimming the waves. Passengers were really getting nervous. What a huge mistake the captain made announcing this triggering a serious emotional disaster for the passengers.

The plane finally landed at Bermuda parking far away from the terminals. But instead of dropping the air stairs so everyone could quickly deplane or deploy the emergency chutes for immediate deplanement so passengers could quickly get off and away from a plane they had been told was threatened to be blown up by terrorists, the captain decided to wait for air stairs to be rolled out to the plane. This created near pandemonium in the passenger cabin with people running up and down the aisle screaming 'Let me off this plane!". This was a serious error by the captain. Once he announced the threat thus creating an emergency, he should have followed through with all emergency procedures just as if an emergency existed in reality.

The air stairs finally arrived after nearly 20 minutes of near hell inside the cabin with passengers nearly running off the plane nearly tripping on the air stairs.

Then, instead of taking the passengers to the terminal on a bus, they were asked to stand away from the plane awaiting inspection to see if there was a bomb aboard.

An hour later, the plane was declared safe with passengers told to reboard. I asked the station manager if all cargo had been inspected including specifically the many liquor boxes which had been delivered from local duty free stores. The answer was no. I then invoked my authority(self appointed) from the airlines main office and ordered reboarding stopped until every liquor box had been opened and each bottle had been inspected making sure the liquid therein was liquor and not liquid looking plastique explosives.

I was told that I was out of my mind until I asked " If you want to blow up a plane and not want to be aboard committing suicide, what better way than delivering a liquor box in the name of a passenger who actually is booked with you safely not aboard? "

When all finally had been inspected and I was told this by the station manager, I gave my OK for passengers to get back on the plane and OK for departure.

Was it my job to intervene in this? Not officially. But it was my job to share my experience from the Holocaust, Cold War and military intelligence to do whatever is required to ensure safety and to rule out nothing possible, even if never before seen happening.

Chairman of 1973
Great Miami Air Race

My title and responsibilities as a manager at Eastern Airlines included community service. I took this seriously and was appointed as Eastern's representative to the Greater Miami Chamber of Commerce. Since I also was an engineer familiar with airplane operations, I was appointed to serve as chairman of the 1973 Great Miami Air Race which had been an annual event carried at the Tamiami General Aviation Airport west of Miami International Airport.

This was an air show consisting of pilots coming from all around the country racing private aircraft of all kinds, vintage, old military and experimental around pylons at the opposite ends of the airport. It was a major event. Just before the event was to start, disaster struck and it was my lucky day to be the Chairman.

The Mideast exploded, the Arab world again went to war against Israel, Egypt closed the Suez Canal and the world experienced "The Oil Embargo". This became a disaster for the Great Miami Air Race of which I just that year happen to be chairman.

The Air Race had to be cancelled never to again be seen in Miami. Instead of being Chairman of the Air Race, I became chairman of Miami Dade County's first Emergency Planning Committee. Instead of dealing with vintage airplanes racing round a field, I had to deal with traffic emergencies resulting from long gas lines, closed gas stations and near transportation chaos with trucks running out of fuel for deliveries and all sorts of things.

President Business Economists Association

As my Eastern title included "Economic Planning" my boss sponsored me to join the South Florida Business Economists Association. This was a group of economists primarily professors from University of Miami, economists from state and county offices and some from banks. Nearly all of them had PhD degrees in economics dealing mostly with economic data and theoretical kind of things.

Membership in the South Florida group required also membership in the National Association of Business Economists Association which had as a requirement to have a degree in economics and preferably an advanced degree. I only had a degree in electrical engineering but when it became known that I somehow had discovered the practical side of business economics, the academic degree requirement was waived and I was accepted as a full member of the NABE.

It wasn't long before I was appointed to committees and in the third year of my membership, I was elected the association's president. This gave me the distinction of being the only person ever being president without a PhD in economics and heading a group of members some of whom would become chief economist of such banks as Bank of America and holding high office at the Federal reserve.

This role even led me to be invited as guest lecturer at Florida International University in economics and to give a short course in business forecasting at University of Miami. It became known that I, as an engineer and former military intelligence specialist had somehow discovered the secret of knowing how to actually use the principles of economics in a business setting.

Land Baron – dream or reality?

I always wanted to create a family legacy so that something of my family would be left to future generations. The idea of building a real estate business while still working then to retire from my regular job eventually handing it to our sons seemed right. It was fairly easy to buy a small house and rent it and then add more houses as the value rose over time using the increased value as the financing needed.

Kenneth, our youngest son seemed to be interested in real estate so we bought our first investment house in 1973 and rented it out. I also took a course in real estate to become a broker and later, as Ken got older, sponsored him also to become a broker. He even got a masters degree in business administration with a real estate major and on graduating, got a job with one of Miami's premier commercial real estate companies to learn the business. Along the way, Shirley & I added to our real estate holdings eventually owning 3 houses, two townhouses and 3 condos to be rented out. Shirley & I were a team. I did the financing and did most of the maintenance and she was the land lady.

One story worth telling is about the townhouse which we rented to a couple with a small child. We checked them out and seemed OK but as we learned later, we hadn't learned enough. The "wife" always paid the rent in cash (a red flag). Then, when one month the wife didn't come with the rent, we went to the place and found it almost empty with a few bullet holes in the garage door. The furniture was gone but some boxes were still in the garage. Going through the boxes we saw wedding pictures of the wife but the husband wasn't the same one we had met.

A second "landlord" story worth telling is about Andrew (not the hurricane). While we were away on vacation, our son hadn't followed our instructions and took a deposit from a black U.S. customs agent working at the airport. We learned that he wanted to rent the condo for himself and his girlfriend as a "trysting place" as he had a wife and kids in a house.

His credit was OK but too high for his pay and under normal circumstances, we would have returned his deposit. But since he was a U.S. customs agent and a minority person. we feared discriminatory problems and rented it to him anyway. How wrong could we go with a U.S, customs agent? Very wrong.

A few weeks after they moved in, we received complaints from neighbors about strong pot odors were coming from the condo. On checking out the place, we found solid evidence that drugs were being used. I gave Andrew the choice of moving out within 48 hours or I would report him to U.S. Customs. Andrew moved out. We lucked out not realizing until a month later how much we did luck out. Reading the Sunday paper, I say to Shirley " Take a look at the paper. There on the front cover of the Miami Sunday Herald we see a picture of Andrew with several other customs agents being escorted from the airport handcuffed. They were arrested for steering drug carriers from South America through the Customs inspection lines and letting them through.

Unfortunately, Ken didn't follow through with his opportunities either on his jobs or as a real estate broker. Eventually, as it became apparent we couldn't hold on the real estate due to some financial difficulties brought about by the "Crash of 87" and Hurricane Andrew, we sold all but the one where Ken lived and still does as of this writing. That ended our dream of having a family real estate business.

The Discovery Letter - 1981

My work in the economics community led me to learn a great deal about investments and the stock market. The word got out that "Gunther" was the guy who knew about the undiscovered tech stocks and the "Discovery Letter" was born. This was a 2-3 page newsletter about economics in terms the average person could understand and a list of just a few, rarely more than five, stocks we ourselves bought. We also created and issued a one page "Research Report" telling the basics of the company with updates in the following monthly "Discovery Letter". Shirley & I did this together with me doing the research and writing and she the editing and helping with circulation.

We decided to make this a proper investment letter, so we advertised it in financial magazines. Before we knew it, the circulation had grown to nearly 3,000 nationally, I was invited to write comments in financial papers, was quoted in the Wall Street Journal and invited to speak at meetings. We were invited twice to speak at a major financial conventions at Caesars Palace in Las Vegas.

This led me to be invited to be a panelist on a TV network show on the Financial News Channel(FNN) which was the predecessor to CNBC. It was "Stocks, Options and Futures" sponsored by the Ira Epstein Brokerage Company in Chicago. The show originated in Chicago at the Merchandise Mart downtown Chicago.

We flew to Chicago to do the program several times and were put up at the famous Palmer House Hotel . The program went out over the FNN, local TV stations and radio stations all over the country. The deal we had was for me to do this free but I could advertise live on the program the "Discovery Letter" offering a trial subscription. The peak occurred when we received about 2,000 requests for trial subscriptions. This was before emails and we had to send the newsletter by U. S. Mail.

We had to get 2,000 copies plus offering materials printed at a local print shop, we had to collate, staple, create envelope labels, paste the labels on envelopes, stuff the envelopes and then paste stamps on the 2000 envelopes. All this was done on our kitchen table.

We started this "business" while I still worked with Eastern with the intent to continue it when I retired. When my Eastern job suddenly ceased along with Eastern Airlines itself far too soon in 1986 we made this our fulltime job.

We kept the Discovery Letter going adapting it to the changing times, emails and the Internet. We met people from all over the world and still maintain contact with some. Right after one of the Chicago TV programs, Jim Walters from Carlsbad Calif. called telling me I had mispronounced the name of his company 'International Totalizator Systems". Jim was its founder and CEO who invited us to visit his company and to this day, over 30 years later, we maintain contact. We met Albert Hanser as Chairman of Hanrow Capital Management, a major investment company in Minneapolis. We have remained good friends to this day and he even has written a comment for this book.

When the stock market collapsed in the "Tech meltdown" of 2001 and 9/11, our subscriptions dried up and we stopped reporting on stocks. But we continued the "Letter" focused on current critical issues on economics, politics and national security telling "What they don't want you to know". We also cancelled the subscription price making it our free public service.

This led to speaking engagements including a two year assignment to speak aboard major cruise ships principally Celebrity Cruises and Radisson Seven Seas.

World Travelers

One of the great benefits of working for an airline and especially in a management position is nearly free air travel throughout the world. Shirley & I took advantage of this as we travelled throughout Europe, Israel, Australia, South Pacific and of course the U.S.

We went to San Francisco just for weekends, New Orleans to visit Shirley's relatives and to weddings all over. We flew to Sweden just for the weekend to attend the Christening of our friend's grandson in Gothenburg. Shirley celebrated her 50th birthday with a banquet just in her honor also hosted by our friends in Gothenburg. This was a formal event starting with a gathering before the dinner, the banquet itself stretching all the way into breakfast attended by dignitaries such as judges, noted artists and a member of the Swedish royal family. This was an event never to be forgotten.

On a trip to Stockholm, friends invited us on their 40 ft. sailboat on a day's trip out of the Stockholm harbor into the archipelago all the way into the Sea of Bothnia which lies between Sweden and Northern Finland. We encountered sudden gale force winds with waves going over the bow and we had to close the hatch. Needless to say, Shirley would never again go on a large sailboat into open sea.

On another trip to Australia(One of three to Australia), we took a high speed catamaran out of Port Arthur to an offshore platform on the Great Barrier Reef about 60 miles offshore. The winds kicked up and with the high speed boat just keeping going hitting the waves, Shirley got sick. A nice lady came over to put a cold towel on Shirley's forehead to comfort her. When she left, a passenger asked Shirley if she know who that was. It was Elizabeth Montgomery, the actress on Bewitched and other TV programs.

A really great trip was our long weekend to Portugal. We left Miami Friday morning on an Eastern flight connecting to a Portugal TAP Airways flight leaving evening for arrival Saturday morning in Lisbon nonstop.

We were awakened about 5 am when the plane landed and we got off thinking we were there. Wrong. The plane had landed in the Azores where at that very time President Nixon was having a summit meeting and the plane delivered wine and dishes for the event. We almost got stranded in Lejes as we had a problem convincing the boarding agent we belonged back on the plane and were going to Lisbon.

Arriving Lisbon, we took a shuttle to a hotel in Estoril, a resort town north of Lisbon where we stayed until Monday for our return. While there, we met a couple, the wife from Chile and husband from Munich, Germany visiting from Long Island. We jointly rented a car and toured the Algarve Coast of Portugal, stopping at a restaurant where we had the best seafood bouillabaisse we'll never forget. On the road, we chanced by a village with a dirt road and huts. A lady invited us inside her house which was a one room hut with no floor and a table made of a half barrel with a white table cloth. She served us a piece of home made very dark bread and a glass of wine. None of us spoke Portugese but thanks to our new friend from Chile who spoke Spanish, we got by. We returned and arrived Miami Tuesday evening.

The grand daddy of all trips

We were scheduled for our second trip to Australia via Tokyo and Fijii Islands and arranged for our sons to visit the farm in Sweden for several weeks. I got the standby tickets for our sons to Sweden and just in case I couldn't get them on the direct flight to Stockholm, I also got myself a ticket. Sure enough, the direct SAS flight to Stockholm was full and the next was a flight with a change in Copenhagen. I didn't think they could change flights in Copenhagen on standby so I got on the flight myself with them flying to Copenhagen where we changed for another flight to Stockholm. In Stockholm, I rented a car and drove the 300 miles to the farm in Dalarna, turned around to Stockholm for a flight to New York. There, I took the next flight to Miami, spent the night at home.

The next morning, Shirley & I got on a nonstop flight to San Francisco where we caught the non stop to Tokyo, spent the night there and then to Fiji where we stayed three days before going on to Australia where our good friends, the Nolte's were waiting for us.

Just think of the time zone changes for this trip in one almost nonstop trip. Thankfully, this was mostly a first class seat trip with great food and service, which today(2014) is a relic of the past.

The beginning of the end of Eastern Airlines

Although Eastern Airlines was one of the pioneering airlines and at one time, the second largest in the USA with over 40,000 employees and 125 stations all over the USA, Latin America and some in Europe, it had been on a financial tightrope for some time. This required a strong financial management policy especially as the entire industry was going through a major deregulation phase. Unfortunately, it had a weak top management team led by an even weaker board which did not much else except to bless whatever the CEO wanted to do.

The CEO was Col. Frank Borman, the revered astronaut who piloted the spacecraft to the Moon. Under his leadership, Eastern struggled for 11 years between 1975 and 1986 when he sold Eastern to Texas Air which subsequently liquidated the company.

I knew Frank personally attending senior executive meetings. Although Frank was an excellent military person as an Air Force colonel and astronaut flying the first astronauts to the Moon, he was severely lacking in corporate management. His total management training consisted of a three month executive school at Harvard Eastern had sent him to after he was hired. His predecessor, Floyd Hall, the primary long term CEO since the founder, Eddie Rickenbacker, had a thing about having to have an astronaut for CEO. After failing with Scott Crossfield who was being groomed for the job and failed as Crossfield couldn't stay away from the bar, Borman became the man. Borman was a great public relations front man but a poor manager of a large company with financial troubles and poor in labor relations with aggressive unions.

Instead of managing by strong management principles, Borman was a good example of managing by '**A wing and a prayer".** He even sponsored "prayer meetings" in the company cafeteria during lunch praying for the company's salvation. Instead of appointing a Chief Financial Officer (CFO) with a strong financial background, he appointed his long time buddy from the West Point Military Academy with a PhD in military science.

Here is one example of serious management missteps. Borman had insisted on being the first to order the French A300 widebody right after the airlines were deregulated in 1979. This added new debt at a time when an already debt laden company should be reducing debt load. Then the cargo vice president comes up with a grandiose scheme of filling the cargo container space with cheap forwarder traffic before doing a cost analysis. This became to be known as the famous "Moonlight Special" with all A300's setting up a hub in Houston to load and transfer air freight for CF Air Freight at night.

Since I was the person responsible for the cargo revenue forecast, it became my job to tell management what the revenues would be and I was told that was decided by a contract to sell the entire belly container capacity for the Houston overnight hub. When I asked what the costs of this were I was told not to worry about that because "Frank" (Borman) would make a deal with the pilots union for reduced pilot costs as a union concession to help the airline. I insisted in waiting to book the revenue to the forecast until this union agreement had been reached and was told that wasn't my business and to trust Frank.

The contract with CF Air Freight for a fixed price was signed before Frank was able to sign the deal for reduced cost with the pilots and indeed, was never signed. Worse still, whoever concocted this deal forgot to add cost for the extra maintenance that would be required to refurbish the airplanes each night after the cargo readying the planes for the daytime passengers.

This turned out to become a huge problem not only in added cost but in passenger cabin condition which caused a loss of passengers. This great deal concocted by Eastern's top management team led by its great colonel contributed about $300 million in losses before the Moonlight Special was grounded. The Moonlight Special was a good idea implemented extremely poorly and a program that illustrated Eastern's poor top management quality.

One of Eastern's best business segments was Airmail contributing to over $100 million in annual revenues from the Post Office. As technology started to offer early versions of electronic mail such as the Western Union Easy Link, I issued a warning of declining Airmail revenues resulting from increasing electronic mail and described what would become today's email. I cited my strong engineering background with myself even pioneering the communications leading to email. But, I was labeled a lunatic who didn't understand that there would always be a solid Airmail business.

This decision violated sound business principles. Today, who uses Airmail instead of email? Do you? The added cost of maintaining the projected high airmail facilities along with the ultimate decline in revenues that occurred became another spike in Eastern's coffin.

Gunther's plan to save Eastern Airlines fails

Frank Borman's "war" with the IAM (International Association of Machinists) and it's leader Charlie Bryan escalated starting about 1984. Although Borman was able to avert a strike by having the unions agree to a pay cut, labor relations worsened.

My title included "Manager of Economic Planning and, although above my paygrade, I decided to invoke my creative ability. I believed that peace between the unions and management might be achieved if the employees owned a part of the company,

This led me to create a plan whereby all employees, union and non union alike would give up raises for three years by accepting Eastern airline stock equivalent to what the raise would have been in exchange for a no strike agreement during this three year period. The company would save about $750 million in actual cash flow savings, a critical amount needed to meet bank loan agreements thus avoiding bankruptcy. Since this would give employees a 20% equity ownership position of Eastern, part of the plan also would be for the employees to be given one board seat. The theory in this plan was to make employees feel they in part were working for themselves and therefore would work harder, smarter and less apt to work against the company by striking as that would be like working against themselves.

Charlie Bryan's(the Union president) financial analyst was a subscriber to our Discovery Letter so I knew the key person in the IAM union office. I discussed this plan with him and reached an agreement that Charlie Bryant and the union would agree with my plan. I presented the plan also to the pilots union and they also agreed to support my plan.

But when I took my plan to my Eastern's senior team, I was told that I hadn't been assigned to develop such plans and that I was out of my mind to even get involved with this and to stick with my forecasts. My boss laughed at me when I told him my next forecast would take Eastern out of business and he threw me out of his office. Frank Borman had made the decision and that was that.

Although this likely will become known as one of the worst decisions a CEO can make, the ultimate responsibility for allowing Borman to make this decision was the board's because it failed to supervise the CEO. The Board represents the owners who are the shareholders and the CEO and all key officers are responsible to the board. This system failed at Eastern Airlines as clearly, the board let Borman do whatever he always wanted and what he wanted violated sound business practices.

I knew then that my days were numbered. Fortunately, my Discovery Letter side business was doing well and I planned to go to it fulltime if and when my Eastern job ended. My hope against hope was to last at least until I was 62 and then retire at full retirement pay and Social Security. However, that was not to be.

The end nears
for Eastern Airlines

The next critical stage in Eastern's declining life came at the quarterly review meeting in the spring of 1986 when I presented my revenue forecast. The financial vice president (Military PhD) said to me "Your revenue is too low. It's below my expenses. Raise it to cover the expenses". Frank Borman looks at me and says, "Yes, do that". My question then became 'Frank, by how much would you want me to raise the forecast?". Frank answered "by whatever the banks need to meet our obligations".

"But Frank, that's a 12 % revenue increase or about $600 million. Where is the money to come from? Are you going to expand operations with more planes, add more seats and cargo capacity and blow wind on a failing economy?", Frank's answer was 'Just raise the forecast to what Wayne (the CFO) needs. My answer "Frank, sorry, but I won't do that because it would be illegal and be called "cooking the books" and I don't want a reservation in a jail cell.

That would be my last meeting with Frank Borman and final forecast I did for Eastern having developed the system and managing it for 15 years.

The end of Eastern Airlines and my corporate career

The date February 28, 1986 at 12:00 midnight is the date Eastern Airlines employees, its shareholders and historians should remember. This was the deadline Frank Borman had given Charlie Bryan and his IAM union to agree to further pay cuts or he would sell the airline to Frank Lorenzo of Texas Air who likely would liquidate the airline. The union agreed to Borman's terms on the condition that he resigns.

Borman then made another serious management error with the board doing nothing to stop him. He in effect told the employees that if he, Frank Borman could not continue leading Eastern, no one should and he sold Eastern Airlines, himself "retiring" along with his team with handsome "golden parachutes" with him personally leaving with $1 million cash.

With Borman and his team gone, Texas Air brought in new managers who eventually filed Chapter 11 bankruptcy eventually leading to the airline shutting down in 1991. People were being laid off until finally, all but a few of the 40,000 employees were gone. It is believed that more former Eastern employees committed suicide than were killed on active duty in the 1991 Gulf War. One of the managers I had worked with hit the bottle, his wife threw him out and the last anyone heard of him he was living out of the trunk of his car.

My end came on the day before Labor Day long weekend in 1986, just a few months after my final revenue meeting. The boss called me in to his office and gave me the termination contract and told me to clear out my office and leave that day. I went back to my office and when turning on my computer to close out my files, I was "denied access". That was the end of my 20 years at Eastern and the coming end of that Airline.

A tragedy in business history, a tragedy in Airline history and worst of all, a huge human tragedy for 40,000 employees and total loss for shareholders.

Did corruption kill Eastern Airlines?

You bet there was corruption but I don't believe that was a significant cause of the failure. I believe the failure was caused by simple mismanagement. The story wouldn't be complete without mentioning at least one juicy story about clear fraud in the corporate suite.

The senior Vice President in charge of planning who also was my boss was also on the board of Centrust Savings Bank and chairman of its executive compensation committee. Centrust Savings was a leading Miami based bank with a president who also was an art lover. The Eastern VP in charge of planning's wife was the art consultant to the president of Centrust getting paid $25,000 per year for buying fine art pieces for the Centrust Savings building and its president's office. This all was happening at the very time when Centrust Bank was raising the funds for Texas Air and Frank Lorenzo to buy Eastern. The president of Centrust was indicted, convicted on unrelated charges, served years in jail and Centrust Savings was liquidated in the Savings & Loan collapse of the late 80's,

Although the collusion between high Eastern officers and Centrust clearly indicated a solid conflict of interest and I disclosed this to the U.S. Attorney at the time, nothing was ever done about this corporate fraud.

The company's personnel department did intentionally try to commit fraud with my pension however. I was laid off just a few months before completing 20 years which significantly reduced my pension. Fortunately, Eastern's attorney was also a subscriber to my Discovery Letter and knew what I was capable of. After a conversation with him, he convinced Eastern's top person to offer a settlement to me and we settled. This included raising my employment to 20 years with health insurance benefits for life.

Gunther The Consultant

Shirley & I had been going to a local temple where we met Steve (not real name for reasons you soon will learn) who became a Discovery Letter subscriber. He was fascinated with my methods of evaluating small companies and told me about his business. Steve had a small consulting group of about a dozen highly paid mostly PhD's in industrial psychology who were supposed to help other companies become more efficient. His company which I'll call the PH Group practiced the principles of famed Dr. Edwards Deming who was the famed industrial engineer sent to Japan and helped it out of its post economic WW II disaster. Dr. Deming created the "Deming Method" of industrial engineering and Steve was one of his students who became his disciple. The PH Group's clients included large corporations such as General Motors, BASF Chemicals and the U.S. Navy with contracts in the millions.

As we got to know each other, Steve complained extensively about problems with his own business and asked me if I would look into his business to find out what was wrong. This would become my next assignment after Eastern and as Eastern did, also turned to disaster.

The office was in North Miami Beach, about 30 miles from where we lived and where Steve lived. Steve had told his secretary to expect me with instructions to show me the office and answer any of my questions.

What faced me when entering the office was the rear of a 300 lb woman sitting behind a cluttered desk with a computer that had wires strung all over and noticeably worn carpet. That was Sherry who ran the office. She introduced me to the accountant who was sitting at a very cluttered desk but no computer. He had retired from somewhere else and hadn't yet discovered computerized accounting doing everything by hand and hadn't yet heard of "accounts receivables" making sure clients paid their bills.

I asked Sherry about the company's travel arrangements because one of Steve's complaints was about problems with hotel and travel for the dozen consultants constantly travelling. She told me that Steve's partner's friend was a part time travel agent who handled all travel. Wow, this was sounding like a real disaster for a business spending over $100,000 annually for travel. Sherry also told me that Steve and the other consultants rarely stop by the office. All this confirmed to me that the PH Group, which was advising major companies on improving efficiency and how to better manage their business, was itself a disorganized business operating near disaster levels.

When Steve asked me what I thought of his office, I gave him the straight facts. It was a disaster and not surprising he was having all the problems he had been telling me about. He asked me what should be done and again I gave him the straight facts. Either move his residence closer to the office so he can go to it regularly to supervise it or move the office so he can go to work on time. I also told him to replace the accountant and travel agents with professionals and computerize his office. It was tough telling the head of a PhD staffed consulting group advising major corporations on efficiency that his own office was a disaster needing a major restructuring.

Steve asked me if I could handle the reorganization, implement it and manage the office so I agreed since the Eastern job had ended and the pay was good. But it was clear that the assignment would be for no more than 80% of fulltime so I could continue my Discovery Letter and investment business.

The first thing I did was find a new and much larger office space near where Steve lived so he could be at work on time when the office opens dressed in something better than jeans and tee shirt. I fired the accountant, bought several computers and accounting software and myself created a proper accounting and office system and then trained a new accountant how to use it. I fired the travel agent replacing her with a professional travel management company.

Shirley helped with all this and we both worked like dogs for nearly a year getting all this done. It was an uphill struggle. Why?

Steve's partner, Dianne resented me coming in redoing the disaster she had created.. Since I had met Steve in the Temple and word got out that I was running his business, I became deluged with business offers by temple members offering insurance, office supplies and a travel agent who believed she deserved the travel account. This became a real problem so we quit the temple because I didn't want to mix religion with business.

But this is the worst. When I set up the accounting system, I noticed that the Rabbi was getting paid thousands of dollars per month and I ran into problems trying to find out what he did so I could assign a correct accounting code for him. I also noticed that Steve's wife was the rabbi's assistant always with him wherever he went. When I also noticed that good looking Dianne, Steve/s partner was almost always taking the same trips staying in the same hotel, I knew I had a problem.

When Dianne learned what I knew she brought in the father of one of the consultants to straighten out the office which I was running and Steve promptly fired me. The interesting thing was that the Consultant's father, Raul, proclaimed to once have been Fidel Castro's Finance Minister in Cuba and was an efficiency expert.

The story doesn't end, yet. I had agreed to work 80% of fulltime being paid for the number of hours based on that. But the assignment actually required me to work 120% of fulltime racking up many overtime hours. So when I got fired, I submitted a bill for the unpaid hours but Steve refused. I sued him for the money owed and learned yet another important principle. What matters is not what's true and the right thing. I discovered the true meaning of the Russian proverb "When money speaks, truth keeps silent" even in the court.

Steve with his money had on retainer for his business a prominent lawyer, the same who defended General Noriega, the former president of Panama in his drug trial. He counter sues me for mismanagement of his office and wins. Not only didn't I get paid my back pay, but I ended up owing him money.

This, along with the Crash of 87 which nearly wiped out our investments eventually forced us to file for bankruptcy to protect our remaining assets from my former great PhD consultant "friend" Steve.

So what's happened to Steve, Diane and us, Gunther & Shirley? Steve's wife divorced him and he eventually married Diane. Steve's business went downhill to just the two of them. The rabbi left the temple and moved away. Shirley & I survived that storm and are today happily still together and getting ready for our 60th anniversary cruise and this new book telling it all. We may not be the millionaires we thought we would become nor live in a mansion on a beach, but we still are "here" at 80 and 81 living well enough.

That was a tremendous learning experience which proved yet another old expression "If you can't do it, teach it "

Gunther hauls corrupt
real estate developer to jail

The phone rang right after the PHG assignment ended with an offer by a real estate developer. It was a small public company with its shares traded on NASDAQ. I won't use its real name for reasons becoming obvious. I'll refer it as TKG.

The TKG president invited me to come in as "Director of Strategic Planning" handling shareholder relations, acquisitions and matters with regulators including SEC filings. The office was downtown in a Brickell Ave building overlooking Biscayne Bay.

TKG owned and was acquiring additional upscale mobile home communities across Florida already owning 10 large properties averaging 1000 spaces each. The business was owning the land, developing it into spaces for manufactured homes, selling the homes to mostly Canadians, leasing spaces and charging for utilities and other services. Accounting was consolidated into the Miami main office which collected the money from all residents across the state.

The company had its own plane with a fulltime pilot which we took to visit the various properties across the state. The president liked Shirley and often invited Shirley to come along and curiously gave her a roll of $20 bills for lunch and shopping while we did the business.

The problem I encountered right away was that the company was excessively leveraged owing too much money it had trouble paying. Contractors were even driving from across the state right to the office to get paid and the president usually was behind closed doors to avoid process servers for creditors suing to get paid.

I told the president that instead of acquiring more properties which is why he hired me, he needed to sell and downsize. I also wanted to find out where all the money was going that was being collected from the properties and not going into maintaining them properly.

That opened up the pandoras box with a story movies are made of. Lots of the money being collected from the tenants across the state was laundered into personal accounts from which the president paid for maintaining race horses at the race track with a fulltime trainer and condos he bought for his family. The company also had excessively high costs as he had appointed his father in law to be vice president(in charge of sitting in his office reading the Wall Street Journal) and his wife who rarely was seen in the office. The company also sponsored lots of political events for politicians and getting tickets for the Miami Heat to give out to friends. Most of these activities were illegal use of corporate funds.

Since the company was a public company with shares trading, the president was very concerned about share prices and spent lots of time dealing with his stock broker. I was responsible for issuing press releases and when it was time to announce the past qtr's financial results, the president told me to include a million dollar profit from the sale of a small piece of land and book it into operating results. I told his financial officer this violates accounting rules and I couldn't make such an announcement. However, I was ordered to issue the release and instead resigned because of not only this, but all the other illegal activities I had uncovered.

Then, I went to the local SEC (Securities and Exchange Commission) office and disclosed what I knew. By the time it and the Justice Dept investigated the company and its president, he was charged with federal indictments for securities fraud, illegal use of corporate funds for personal use and tax evasion. He was arrested, convicted and given a prison sentence. The company was closed down and filed for bankruptcy. Fortunately for me, I also was a licensed real estate broker and sold a $11 million upscale mobile home community and collected my commission.

This was to be the beginning of a long term interest in rooting out corporate fraud leading to my first book "Thieves on Wall Street".

Gunther The Stock Broker

The Discovery Letter increasingly led me into the financial services industry eventually getting the SEC Investment Advisors license as I always wanted to be in compliance with all regulations. Realizing that I should get all licenses to get paid for all services, I became a licensed stock broker and even went as far as getting the brokerage principal license qualifying me to become a branch office manager of a brokerage house. This required me to take extensive courses, attend classes and pass very tough tests administered by the NASD (National Association of Securities Dealers, now FINRA).

Once getting all these licenses, I set up my office in the house including computers with quote screens and access to immediate newswires and a relationship with a broker dealer so I could handle transactions for clients. This led me to become branch manager of a California brokerage company which invited me to attend an all expense paid three day meeting in San Diego. I even became the State of Florida compliance officer for the California brokerage company and its South Florida instructor for people wanting to learn the brokerage business and pass the tough NASD exam.

I maintained all my securities industry licenses until 1995 when I retired them so I could expose the truth about the stock market, its traders and all those people perpetrating fraud mostly against the individual shareholder. Holding an active license requires being affiliated with a securities firm and all written materials issued to clients must be approved by the firm. Which firm would have approved the publishing of my first book "Thieves on Wall Street"?

The Crash of 87 was a Disaster

In one week, the market crashed 35% with most of the loss happening on Black Tuesday, October 19, 1987. Investors trying to sell stocks to raise cash not knowing how far down it would go couldn't because the brokers didn't pick up their phones. Over the next week, margin calls triggered by the huge loss in value wiped out many investors. One trader went to the Merrill Lynch brokerage office near our house on a shooting rampage rendering its manager a cripple for life.

The "Crash" nearly wiped out our own portfolio and did destroy our Discovery Letter as a business because investors no longer renewed their subscriptions. However, as a moral obligation to my subscribers, we continued publishing our Discovery Newsletter to update them on what was happening with their stocks and the market. We did however gradually shift the focus to telling the truth about Wall Street , corrupt CEO's and bad politicians. The Discovery Letter continues to be published as of the issue of this book, now for 33 years as our public service without charge. I wouldn't be surprised if it is not the longest published such "Letter" in history.

We handed it out during our many seminars and lectures at meetings, on the cruises I was invited to be speaker on and facilitated several lecture series on corporate responsibility and shareholder rights. In fact, we announced this book in a Discovery Letter issue which for years has been only electronically delivered.

Gunther Karger

The scam boutique 1991-92

I was invited to set up my office within the Sun Business Group which was a building of individual offices occupied by individuals. The system was that each person was to contribute his share of income from a completed transaction with all within the group cooperating on deals. I was the only person doing business as a stock broker providing quotes and financial data from my computer system which I brought to the office.

I quickly learned that this should be called the 'Sun Fraud Center" because that's what it was. No transaction was ever completed to the best of my knowledge. The deals were typically megadeals often in the billions of Dollars and yes, I did say Billion. The "propositions" invariable had to do with brokering various things cooperating with other brokers with each broker getting a piece of the commission. This was before email existed so all communications were handled on the phone with documents via fax.

This business was nearly entirely based on introductions which became more the product than the deal itself so the identity of introductions was closely guarded until a nondisclosure agreement was signed and communicated via fax. There were times when as many as ten "brokers" were connected on a "string" telephone call with each "introducing" the other discussing the details of the deal.

The propositions ranged from tons of gold reaching into hundreds of Million dollars, Kuwaiti Dinars (currency) in the billions, ships full of cement and yes, once there was a ship of tons of frozen chicken. Crude oil was also a favorite commodity. The interesting thing was that these were not futures contracts but the actual physical product someone claimed he had for sale and someone claimed he had a buyer for. In all these 'deals" I never "met" anyone actually owning anything offered for sale.

They all were "introducing brokers" each sharing commissions and each marking up the price for the next broker. These people didn't know it but they in effect were creating a giant Ponzi Scheme since at the bottomline of all this there was never anything "there". I never once saw single deal close with money exchanged.

A favorite scheme was the "Prime Bank Guarantee" known as the PBG roll. This was a favorite means of raising funds for a business deal. The structure was that the difference between the interest offered by the issuing bank and the buyer of the "bond" became the fee received by the brokers and often there were many introducing brokers to receive a piece of the fee. All this was confirmed after the introduction telephone call by a signed fax. These PBG were called rolls because once started, they were designed to keep "rolling" in what became known as bank tranches.

I'll never forget one such "deal" which as they all usually did, involved Zurich, Switzerland based money or gold stashes somewhere in a Swiss vault. The Sun Business brokers consisting principally of two partners and one's father-in-law were in the office at 3 am which was 9 am Zurich time when Swiss business opens, all waiting for the deal to close. The two Sun brokers who also claimed to own the building were so sure they would close the deal making millions that they had actually gone to the Miami Beach Rolls Royce dealer and picked out the colors of the Bentley for each of them. The Father in law had made an appointment with me to discuss which investments he should make with his cut of the millions. I even participated in this "deal" because I provided the market information from my computers. For one week, we came in at 3 am having coffee and donuts waiting for the deal to close. The missing piece was the "banking coordinates" (bank routing and account numbers) of the 'seller" which only the originating broker had (the broker who claimed to personally know the seller).

The end came when he was tracked down to a phone booth in Scotland and he said that he didn't have the bank coordinates after all. This collapsed the deal, everybody on the telephone "string" yelled at each other threatening to kill whoever was responsible.

The Sun brokers cancelled their Rolls Royce car and the Father in Law committed suicide. One of the Sun brokers came into my office and ripped out my computer and basically evicted me. The Sun Business Group collapsed because they couldn't pay the massive phone and fax bill that had racked up. Remember, this was during the era when long distance calls were expensive and some of these were overseas calls. The Sun Group eventually went bankrupt not being able to pay the huge telephone and fax bill, lost the building and left town to start their sunshine "business" elsewhere.

The "crème de la crème" deal came to me when Ackbar called me form Houston offering me a billion Dollars worth of Kuwaiti Dinars for sale. He had heard that I had strong connections with buyers for this product. Ackbar claimed to be associated with the King of Saudi Arabia having worked in the King's office. Just to check out Ackbar, I called Nizzar to check out Ackbar. I had "met" him on one of those phone calls and he claimed to be the nephew of the Saudi king's financial advisor living in Switzerland. Nizzar confirmed that Ackbar was real and yes, he had worked for the Saudi king in Saudi Arabia. But Nizzar also told me that Ackbar's job in the royal court was to procure blond western women for the king and his princes and had once procured bad merchandize and for that was fired and put into exile.

Another interesting deal was the hotel deal in Grenada. This was Jack who was manager of a Miami home for the blind and was raising money to buy a Grenada hotel with money raised from one of the PBG rolls. The deal was to close in a New York bank and Jack actually flew there to close that deal. But no, it didn't happen. But this was the only deal I actually got paid something. Jack's girlfriend was the manager of the Miami Ballet and had given us free tickets to the ballet. So yes, we did get paid but in ballet tickets.

I decided to give this "chapter of my life" detail because I did experience this (and much more) and this truth is probably more interesting read than some fiction.

This chapter, along with more yet to come, illustrated the struggle I had to keep my commitment to provide for my family which I believe is a prime responsibility for a husband.

A final note. The PBG rolls were declared illegal and fraud since they also were a Ponzi Scheme. Some of the "brokers" were arrested and charged by the FBI.

Gunther "the boiler room broker"

The end of the Sun Business Group meant that I had to move all business back to the house where one room was outfitted as an office. My income was derived entirely from the modest pension from Eastern Airlines and a dwindling amount from the Discovery Letter subscriptions. This led me to operate our "business" as a hedge fund creating a portfolio which had the potential of adding to our retirement income. While this kept me busy and involved with the investment world which continued "telling" me how corrupt it was and how extremely difficult it was for the individual investor.

To this was the increasing daily complaint by Shirley that "I have taken her house away" and that I should go out and get a real job. One day, Shirley gave me an ad insisting I answer it.

This led me to a commodities trading broker and my introduction to a real boiler room. The product was futures which required me to get a license allowing me to sell futures contracts for commodities such as metals, pork bellies, crude oil. After getting a real quick training and passing the futures license exam, I was placed in the boiler room and told to do whatever was required to sell generating commissions. This became a real learning experience and invaluable as input to my first book "***Thieves on Wall Street".*** And there was then no doubt "Wall Street" was rampant with thieves and "wolves" running after everybody's hard earned money. I would be remiss not mentioning that this happened 20 years before the movie came out "The Wolf on Wall Street".

Working in this boiler room operation lets me tell you how things work in such a place from first hand experience. The "boiler room" was the second floor of an office building with one open office with about 200 cubicles along two aisles. At front was a raised platform with a podium where the "Research Director" directs the operation.

First, he gives the daily morning "lecture" telling all brokers which product to sell that day. His "research" was mostly clippings form the Wall Street Journal" and he had no clue about much else.

Second, he had headphones listening in on broker calls to "clients" often prompting individuals on how to "close the deal". The "brokers" sat in a cubicle along an aisle with just enough room for stool, board in front with room just with a telephone, a rolodex and a pad. The rolodex was provided with telephone numbers that were to be 'cold called" with a daily quota of 100 per day. Of course, the brokers were strongly encouraged to also call their relatives and friends offering them the tremendous opportunity of making a killing.

The client had no chance at all making money but was nearly guaranteed to lose all his investment. Why? The commission of buying and selling the investment was 40% which meant that the investor had to make a 40% profit just to break even. Second, the investment typically were options on futures contracts whose values fluctuated daily like waves on a stormy sea and expired to zero value sometimes in days. Actual statistics for such operations showed that 99% of all investors in such products lose 100% of their money. But the brokerage house made out like bandits and that they were.

What was happening with the broker in the next cubicle tells the story. He was a refugee from a large well respected real brokerage house where he failed to meet his quota. In one of his cold calls, he "met" a woman who had $6,000 saved to buy a small business but needed $12,000 for the downpayment. The broker convinced her to send her $6,000 in a Fedex envelope to be provided the next morning and that $6,000 would become $12,000 in no time at all. Unfortunately for her, the $6000 instead of exploding to $12,000 in "no time at all" crashed to near zero in even less time. She lost it all but the brokerage house made the 40% commission with a piece going to the broker.

In the eight weeks I was there, I learned a great deal about what happens on "Wall Street". The end came when I quit before getting fired for not meeting my quota. I was lucky. This experience became a chapter in the book I would write "Thieves on Wall Street".

Gunther "the car salesman"

So I came back home to settle back in my "home office" back to the business that I had continued to operate while serving in the boiler room. It wasn't long before Shirley again reminded me that I was occupying "her house" and I needed to get out to get a real job. She gave me a new lead she had seen in the classified jobs section in the paper and insisted I at least look into it. The ad just said "Job opportunity for great money".

The opportunity was for a car salesman and a one week free training class. So for one week, I attended a class learning how to sell cars. What I did learn was that I probably wasn't to be the world's greatest car salesman but I did graduate and was assigned to a Plymouth (discontinued car) and Buick showroom.

Reporting for "work" at 8:00 am, I was shown the back room with about a dozen sales people waiting to be called to the front car showroom when a customer comes in the front door. We were instructed to never, ever, let a prospective customer leave the showroom without first introducing that customer to the "desk manager". What did the desk manager do? He offered to reduce the price down by subtracting the deduction from the salesman's commission. If a sale was made, the salesman(I) would get $25 for selling the car.

After realizing how this system actually worked and that the salesman would be called up front taking turns behind a dozen sales people, I also realized that I would be lucky to sell one car per day being guaranteed $25 per day with the desk manager working against the sales people. That was a non starter for me.

What did I do at lunch time, that first day on the job as a car salesman? I quit and went home for lunch telling Shirley I was "home for good".

That was my one week plus a half day at work of my car sales career which included one week training and a half day at work quitting before selling even one car.

Gunther Karger

Hurricane Andrew August 1992

I had gone to the nearby video store to rent a movie for the weekend. The movie "Hurricane" about the famous typhoon that wiped out Hong Kong in the prior century seemed interesting and we saw it Friday night, not knowing we would somehow have to survive the very next night the worst hurricane ever to hit the United States. Hurricane Andrew.

This storm was expected to have a different track but for some reason, it suddenly picked up dramatic strength and headed straight for our neighborhood. I did what I could putting up a few boards on the windows and taking lawn things into the garage and drained the pool a little.

Then it hit in the middle of that Saturday night, the night after we had seen the movie about a hurricane that destroyed Hong Kong. The winds were so strong that I had to stand behind the front door which was buckling inwards with water streaming horizontally straight through into the living room. The window in bedroom cracked with water streaming in. We were very lucky for the roof not to have blown off.

The next morning, after the storm had "left", we had to dig ourselves out of the house. Our half acre of trees were all down with pieces blocking the front door, a tree branch had fallen on the garage roof crashing through and the pool was full of tree branches and a patio roof that had flown in from a nearby house. Outside, there was not one of our 35 trees standing, all leaves had been stripped from trees and shrubs and the street had turned into a river.

We learned that we had been inside the storm's northern eye wall with winds clocked nearby at 175mph and there were several tornadoes nearby. Many houses had been gutted as the doors blew in lifting off the roofs from the inside.

A few days later, the national guard came with water and soon, a few restaurants opened street kitchens with free food. The insurance company put a trailer on the highway offering emergency money and help with claims.

We cleared out the debris from our house and moved it to the street where bulldozers came in a few weeks moving the debris onto heavy trucks.

It took us a year and $100,000 to repair our house and restore our "jungle" half acre. I called Hurricane Andrew "Andrew the angel" because I used the $100,000 from the insurance company to do much of the repair work myself leaving a significant amount to restore the Discovery Hedge Fund" portfolio.

One hurricane story worth memorializing is the story of Armando, "the contractor" who our lawyer friend Gary introduced us to who could help us rebuilding the house. After getting a $4,000 deposit for replacing the roof and nothing was happening for too long, I investigated him. Surprise!. He wasn't a contractor after all, having "borrowed" the roofer's license. He was a convicted cocaine drug dealer out on bail pending appeal. I made one call and he again took residency in jail.

The roofer still was on the hook for replacing our roof but he never got the deposit from the "'contractor". I gave him the choice of either replacing the roof doing quality work with me personally being the inspector or he too would be going to jail. He opted for the roof, stayed out of jail and our roof lasted for 20 years until we sold the house. Our lawyer friend? He closed his law office (out which the contractor worked) and moved to New Zealand.

Gunther Karger

The day I died, 12/02/1993

The stress of the aftermath of the hurricane and making a living while dealing with family issues apparently were more than my body could handle. In October, 1993, while Shirley was out shopping, I suddenly had sharp chest pains and ended on the kitchen floor. I managed to get up, to the car and drove to nearby hospital about a mile away.

I was given a nuclear stress test to determine the problem as I apparently didn't have a heart attack. In the middle of the stress test, the nuclear scanner failed and I was taken by ambulance to Mount Sinai hospital on Miami Beach. There, I was given an emergency angiogram (running a catheter up into the body looking for blockages) and told I had a spastic artery and was given a vasodilator medicine. After three days in the, hospital, the doctors came into my room telling me that they aren't sure about the diagnosis and want to do the angiogram all over, again. I agreed that maybe that might be necessary but not by them because this should never have to be redone. I checked myself out of the hospital and saw a different cardiologist who did say I really needed a angiogram to find out my problem. I agreed and on December 2, 1993, early in the morning I was scheduled to have it done at Cedars Hospital downtown Miami.

Early that morning with Shirley and Ken, our youngest son in the hospital room, I was being prepared for the angioplasty. As told to me later, it appeared that I had died after the nurse injected the sedative. The 'Blue Code" team was called to try reviving me. I had suffered cardiac arrest, had stopped breathing and was clinically "dead". The error was attributed to a language problem the nurse not clearly understanding the doctor's orders.

Since I am "here" to tell this story, I thankfully survived. Sure enough, there indeed was a blockage in one artery which was causing my chest pains and the other two doctors had missed. Challenging these doctors caused me to be very proactive about medical situations and advise.

Lots of Lox Deli

Lots of Lox is a New York style deli near the house we lived in for 41 years. While I worked observing office hours, Shirley & I walked to it for breakfast on weekends. During the 20 years I worked out of our house office, the Deli became our morning walk and breakfast place.

Over all these years, we met many people with a few remaining good friends even after we moved in 2011 one of these being George & Pam Tabor who we see often even since we moved to Homestead, about 15 miles to the south.

One of the longest Deli employee is Laurie who we met when she was 19 years old and today is in her 40's. Shirley gave her a bridal shower right in the deli when she got married and we all went to her wedding.

We had book signing events at the Deli for our two books, had business meetings and the deli became known as the Palmetto Bay gathering place for politicians. If you wanted to know what's going on, the deli was the place. The Deli as the place became known as, also was the place where Shirley gave many presents to the little children who over the years and all over the world became Shirley's "ersatz" grand children, not having any of her own.

Shirley being the friendly person she is, became the center piece as many people came to breakfast there just to be with 'Shirley ".

Then we moved south to Homestead and discovered Bobbie Joe's, a country style diner where Shirley started to gather her new "flock". The new waitress became Terry and as of 2014, three years after moving to Homestead, Shirley has her new regulars and now, she has me playing "Oh Susanna" on the harmonica for the farm kids.

This book wouldn't be complete without mentioning "Lots of Lox" in Palmetto Bay and now, Bobbie Joe's.in Homestead.

Gunther the Politician

Although I had been involved with IEEE politics running and winning elections for engineering society leadership positions, my introduction to public politics happened while we lived at Cape Canaveral. As Chairman of the IEEE there, I became involved with the election congressman Lou Frey as local campaign chairman. He won serving several terms and, when he ran for Forida governor, our house in Miami was his local campaign Hq.

About 1972, when it was announced that an expressway would be built going right through our great and quite neighborhood, I helped organize a civic association of I served as president defeated the expressway plans. I served as president and in other roles over a period of 30 years and, when the neighborhood became a city, I served on the commission which organized the police department.

When the mayor whom I had supported ran for county commission in 2010 and went against policies I endorsed, I switched my support to his opponent Lynda Bell, the former Homestead Mayor who won by a slim margin. During the past several years, I have become sort of an "oracle" whom politicians seek guidance and endorsement from. As of the writing of this book, I continue making public statements concerning political issues which occasionally are seen in the appears and on TV as shown below appearing on Miami FOX Channel.

Thieves on Wall Street

My long time involvement in all kinds of aspects of Wall Street seeing how badly so many ordinary people were screwed led me to write "Thieves on Wall Street"(1995). The fundamental principle underlying this book was the old Russian proverb I found *"When money speaks, truth keeps silent"* Another focus of this book is to illustrate the insidious "*conflict of interest*" upon which the financial services industry is structured.

Once I decided to write this book, I just got with it and did it. It came straight from my mind, my own recollections making sure all the processes described were technically correct via direct references to industry practices and actual cases. I worked round the clock, mostly through the night. From start to running off the presses, it took six months which may be a record in getting a book done from start to release.

We, Shirley & I, did everything. Shirley was the editor checking for spelling etc. I designed the cover and the sole illustration which I'll include herein but did hire an artist to give both the finish touch.

The Thieves on Wall Street

Investor's World

© Copyright 1995 by Discovery Group, Inc.

Thieves on Wall Street

The cartoon at left illustrates the various investment "things" Reaching out for the pockets of investors. These include the market makers, boiler rooms, brokers, short sellers and all the rest burning your money. This single cartoon illustrate the "Thieves on Wall Street" telling the essence of the story. We created a real publishing company, Discovery Group, Inc. organized as a Nevada company in Reno, Nevada to protect us from liability in case some of the thieves we presented would sue us.

Since this was before the days of electronic publishing, we hired a book printing company to print 3000 copies which delivered the books to our garage. Then, we spent a huge effort marketing the book using press releases and contacting TV and radio hosts. One day, the CNN satellite truck shows up with a reporter who just came from interviewing Fidel Castro in Cuba and I ended up on the CNN right from our own living room. I also appeared live on radio shows from the studio and via telephone taking questions from listeners calling in. "Thieves on Wall Street" launched a new career.

We organized book signings at book stores including Borders, Barnes & Nobles, Books & Books and of course, at our favorite Lots of Lox deli. Beyond selling the books, "Thieves on Wall Street" brought in a consulting deal with a major New York investor relations firm bringing $500 per month for nearly two years.

The most exciting benefit was the invitation to be principal speaker and lecture aboard major cruise ships including Celebrity Cruises and Radisson Seven Seas. This lasted about 3 years and we met many people some of whom we still maintain contact. Shirley was so excited and was n her seventh heaven going first class all the way.

On the tenth anniversary of writing 'Thieves on Wall Street', I wrote its sequel focused primarily on corporate fraud committed more by CEO's and top executives than the brokerage industry. This second book established me as an authority on Wall Street and corporate fraud involving public corporations leading to more speaking invitations.

This is the book that tells you "*The truth they don't want you to know*". It tells CEO's lie about their company's financial reports and how they twist financial reports to make you believe things are great when they stink. The book also tells how the government deceives you by twisting the truth. I am including actual cases where I was personally involved.

Gunther the Cruise Ship Lecturer

While on a two week cruise aboard Celebrity cruises "Infinity" from Florida to San Diego via the Panama Canal about 2003, we were invited to the Captain's formal "dinner". Dinner with the Captain of a major cruise ship is an experience to be remembered. It was during the "formal night" which means that all dinner attendees are required to dress up preferably in formal attire. I wore my white dinner jacket and Shirley her long gown she had bought previously in Barbados.

The captain (Captain Koskinas) had learned that we were booked on his ship and when we checked in for the cruise at the Ft. Lauderdale Port Everglades, we were told we had been upgraded to a suite including a butler, living room and bedroom. It appeared that my reputation had preceded us.

We received a formal invitation to the "Captain's dinner" and asked to meet in one of the lounges for cocktails etc and meet the ship's official hostess. Then, the hostess led us to the grand entrance stairs leading down to the main dining room and as a group of ten guests, to the official Captain's table in a ceremonious walk and personally seated by the Maitre'D. Shirley was given a rose and we were seated next to the Captain. This was a far cry from the 1946 Atlantic crossing on the Gripsholm as a war refugee confined to bottom level steerage class.

The dinner was more like a full course banquet with wine and creative desserts. The "event" and I chose to call this dinner more as an "event" than just a dinner took about two hours and we will never forget it for what it was including the great food. During the dinner and conversation with the captain and other guests, the Captain asked me if I would consider coming "aboard" as a "cruise Lecturer" speaking about the "Thieves on Wall Street" and I of course said that would be great. He gave me the name of the person at the cruise lines HQ to call and said he would brief the person in charge of ship entertainment.

This was the beginning of three years of lecturing aboard Celebrity Cruises. We were called to cruise on the average of a cruise per month and went on every ship Celebrity had visiting nearly all Caribbean and West Coast ports several times. It was a great experience and we met lots of people some of whom we have kept in contact via the "Discovery Letter", our occasional report on current issues and investment fraud.

When the assignment with Celebrity Cruises ended, I was invited to lecture aboard the Radisson Seven Seas "Mariner" which was that cruise lines small luxury ship. The assignment was a two week cruise from Florida via Panama Canal to Lima, Peru from which we were flown back as the ship continued on round South America.

Gunther meets Attorney General

I met U.S. Attorney General John Ashcroft (President George Bush's Attorney General) at a conference on "Economic Crimes of the 21st Century held at St. Thomas University in Miami July, 2006.

One day, the phone rings and it's Russell Spatz, a recently retired Assistant State prosecutor inviting me to attend a two day conference on economic crimes for the 21st century. This was a meeting of mostly prosecutors, judges, state attorney generals and law professors numbering about 100. I was the only non attorney invited because of my reputation for educating and upholding the rights of shareholders of public corporations. John Ashcroft, former Missouri governor, U.S. Senator and Attorney General under President George Bush's first term led a seminar at which he cited me for telling the public the truth about Wall Street and what investors need to know about the inherent conflict of interest that continues to exist.

This event was a highlight of my life having arrived to the U.S. in 1946 as a penniless war orphan and holocaust survivor. To me, this was one of the most significant things I achieved in my entire career because it illustrates that some one as insignificant as me can make some meaningful contribution.

Historic return to my birthplace

In the summer of 2003, I received an email from Edith Dubois in Germany inviting me to a reunion of the holocaust survivors from my hometown which now includes Kippenheim, the town next to Schmieheim. The invitation was extended on behalf of the Burgermeister (mayor) Willi Mattis and it was an all expense paid trip for two weeks including air fare. I agreed if Shirley could also be invited and that was acceptable,

So off we went on Swissair nonstop to Zurich, Switzerland where Edith would pick us up in her car to drive us the short distance across the German border to Kippenheim where we would stay in its best downtown hotel.

Among the approximate 20 survivors and their spouses were Inge Auerbacher from New York who had "discovered" me several years before at a Holocaust survivors convention. Inge was sitting behind a desk selling her books about herself and the holocaust when she noticed my name tag said "Schmieheim, Germany" as all conference attendees had tags with their names and where we were from. She suddenly stood up and shrieked "Impossible!". "Are you the "Gunter who escaped from Schmieheim and fled to Sweden?". "I am indeed that one". This chance meeting led Inge to email Pastor Mattias Krepling, the Schmieheim church pastor who also was head of the local historical society looking for survivors. That became my re- connection to Schmieheim, my hometown.

The two week stay was both memorable and emotional. We visited my family house which had been bought and restored from its rubble. We were invited in for coffee and cake. The owner gave us a bottle of wine he had brewed in the basement where he had a still. The label on that bottle "100 Schlossstrasse" was the first time I had ever seen and known the address of my ancestral home.

Standing next to my restored ancestral home now owned by a person who bought it from the German government for $500 in 1952 and restored it from the rubble it had become. The home had been simply taken from my family by arresting everyone and deporting them to the concentration camp in France. I filed a claim for the house but received nothing because bank charges had used up all remaining funds.

I was invited to address the city council by the mayor(left) and Edith Dubois at right translated my speech to German. This was a historic event as I was the last known Jewish survivor from this town of the deported families and presumed dead. This event was reported in newspapers all over southwestern Germany and filmed by Evelyne Dreyfus of Paris who produced a documentary film about this historic event titled "The Ghosts of Kippenheim".

We were treated to the greatest Black Forest German food on earth. With desserts defying imagination. Edith took us on a personal tour of the Black forest and then back to Zurich for our return flight to Miami.

Shirley & I were invited to a townhall meeting at the Hanna Baumann Kindergarten School named for Hannah Baumann(see my German history chapters) at which I told my story to the towns people and the students. Present were three persons who were in my kindergarten class in Schmieheim and who remembered me. Shirley had a wonderful time being with these exceptionally beautiful children. Also present was the retired postmaster who received my toys from my parent's home after they were deported. Shirley asked him to return the toys but they had long since been lost.

Burgermeister Willy Mattis(with Shirley) personally took us to Europa Park, a disneyland sized theme park nearby on the Rhine River spending the entire day showing us aroumd. On arrival, the park owner, the Baroness, came out of her home, a 600 year old castle to greet us.

Our 50th Anniversary in Paris

Our new friend, Evelyne Dreyfus of Paris who did the documentary French film about our return to Germany insisted we come to Paris for a week to celebrate our 50th Anniversary December 5, 2004. This was an absolute great adventure including seeing the Versailles, Louvre and most of all, the great food in Paris.

A highlight of our Paris visit was meeting Dr. Gottfried Wagner and his wife Teresita from Milan, Italy who our hosts had invited for dinner. Dr. Wagner is none other than the great great grandson of German opera composer Richard Wagner for whom I played on the harmonica, The Overture to the Tannheuser" by Richard Wagner. Gottfried's father was the music director of the famous Beyreuth Music Festival in Germany and whose grandmother was Hitler's social secretary.

Gottfried Wagner unlike his family is not a Nazi. On the contrary, he is a friend of the Jews having written books about the Wagner family.

I am forever thankful to Evelyne for making this memorable trip possible.

Shirley's Doll Museum

In the beginning of this book, I said this is about "us" as Shirley has been part of it for 60 years as of this writing. Shirley came with "dolls" and built her collection to the point at which she had about 2,000 dolls and I felt we lived in a "doll house".

During one of the LSU Miami chapter annual crawfish festivals held always at Tropical Park in the spring, Dr. Charlie Roberts, president of the LSU Alumni Association was in town from the Baton Rouge campus and visited our house. When he saw Shirley's dolls all over our house, he said " Shirley, we have to make a home for your dolls on the LSU campus. We'll build a museum where children can enjoy your dolls forever. We told him "If you do that, we'll donate all the dolls to the museum and create a Gunther and Shirley Karger Scholarship to be funded by 70% of our estate on our death. We all agreed and even signed legal papers to assure this would happen.

This idea of a museum for Shirley's dolls eventually became a reality when in 2005 a major $35 million alumni complex including a hotel, conference center and museum was completed on the LSU campus in Baton Rouge, La.

We shipped the first dolls to establish permanent the exhibit and Shirley had the grand opening of the dolls in 2007 when Shirley's friends and relatives came from New Orleans.

Shirley with her school friends and relatives from New Orleans standing in her doll museum and in friont of the museum building with a massive tiger. She was in her glory which should be recorded in this book.

We visited the LSU campus often staying at the hotel right next door to the museum and enjoying the great Cajun foods of Louisiana. Then, Tom Continue, the original museum director who along with Kelly Poche, a graduate design student designed and created the doll exhibit left. He was replaced by Bud Johnson who had no interest in the dolls because he was only focused on football, the LSU Tigers and sports. That was the beginning of the end of Shirley's doll exhibit.

In the fall of 2013, after we had sold our big house and downsized to a smaller house in Homestead and after the world witnessed the worst economic crisis since the depression house values falling dramatically, the end arrived.

Dr. Charlie Roberts, the LSU Alumni Association long time president and our good longtime friend for over 20 years called to tell us the doll exhibit no longer could remain in the museum. Although Charlie said the primary reason was that the sports exhibits would be moved to the Tiger stadium, he also acknowledged that our financial circumstances had declined and the university was tightening its budget. I reminded him of the written agreement we both had signed ten years before but he argued that we had violated that agreement by not maintaining our financial level evidenced by downsizing to a smaller house.

After an exchange of emails which became more and more formal, it became obvious that Shirley & I didn't die soon enough for Charlie Roberts, LSU Alumni Assoc president and our long time friend to collect our estate before it became depreciated by the financial crisis of 2007-2009. We weren't worth keeping in the LSU family. The bottom line to this was that our service to the world and contributions to make it a better one well recognized nationally was worth much less than money.

We all agreed at the end to terminate all contractual obligations with LSU for the museum and the scholarship and that LSU ship back to us the entire collection. One day, a FEDEX truck came unloading a container of the exhibit which I then reinstalled onto new shelves in our new house.

I also created a website for Shirley's dolls **www.shirleysdollcove.com.** We hope to find a new permanent home for Shirley's dolls so that children can continue enjoying her dolls far beyond our ascendancy to the world beyond. This situation has unfortunately evolved resulting from us not having sons able to take over the collection nor grand children for future generations.

Gunther – The "doctor"

It was 1953 at Chanute Air Base in central Illinois where I was assigned to set up the Air Force weather radar school. The base doctor learned of my electronic training at Keesler AFB (Miss) and asked if I could possibly look at his EEG instrument and calibrate it. An "EEG" is an electroencephalograph device which measures brain waves and does this by attaching many electrode sensors to the head creating a graph read by the doctor. Calibration is critical and that's what the doctor asked me to do. I learned all about how it works, how to calibrate it and just did it. That was my first introduction to medical science.

The next time I addressed medical things was when I wrote the article "Communications in the Year 2000" in 1967 which appeared in "Today's Times" (the forerunner to USA Today). Therein, I included a paragraph describing "medical telemetry" based on the telemetry I had developed for the first communication satellite while in that business in New Jersey. I am told that this might have been the first public reference to "telemetry" in the medical world with telemetry eventually becoming increasingly commonplace over the years.

Five years later, about 1972, while laying in a Miami hospital for a week being evaluated for a thyroid condition the doctors couldn't figure out, I got a pad of paper and drew out what a complete medical telemetry system should look like and what it could do. One nurse asked if I was a doctor.

Shirley had her annual mammogram February 1999 and whammo…there was a problem. Breast cancer had come into our midst. Over the next six months, we endured the worst of surgery, chemo and radiation ..Shirley undergoing it and I taking care of her. The chemo got so bad that twice I had to literally carry her into the hospital for blood transfusions and she almost didn't make it. But, she made it!

I had "met" Dr. Larry Brilliant in connection with a stock deal around 2003. Although at the time, he was CEO of a Silicon Valley based early Internet access company, he was previously a noted epidomologist who was credited with eradicating small pox from India and China in the sixties. A few years later, Larry called me asking if he could show his mother Shirley's doll collection. His mom lived in Hollywood, Florida and he would pick her up on his way back from a meeting in New York on his way back home to San Fransisco.

Larry's business in NYC was a one to one meeting with former Soviet president Mikhail Gorbachev discussing missing small pox virus containers from Russian labs and concern about terrorists might have been able to steal these. Smallpox is a very significant bioterror threat which most people aren't aware of and probably better off not knowing much about it. I have maintained communications with Dr. Brilliant who until recently was Executive Director of the Google Foundation and most recently in 2014, President of Skoll Global hreats Inc. which is concerned with global biological warfare threats.

One night in 2007, Shirley woke up with terrible stomach pains and I took her straightaway to Baptist hospital emergency room. It was a gallbladder attack and the gallbladder had to be removed. While she was in the ER getting checked out, the lung x-ray showed something in the lung which didn't belong. The gallbladder was removed and after extensive tests, it was clear Shirley had a large something in one lung. She needed to have a surgeon take a sample of it to determine what it was.

The cancer doctor, same as had treated Shirley for the breast cancer problems 8 years before said she had to have chemo right away, even before the sample was taken and examined for what kind of tumor she had. I asked the surgeon who would extract the sample if he could remove the entire tumor instead of just a piece for examination. He could and against the advice of the cancer doctor but on my instruction, the surgeon successfully removed a large lymphoma successfully(along with one third of one lung). The doctor used the latest in video assisted thoracic surgery techniques.

After the surgery, the cancer doctor again strongly recommended the chemo but I wanted to defer it until further tests were done to determine if there were any cancer cells remaining after the surgery.

About six weeks after the lung surgery, Shirley developed a nagging worsening cough which didn't go away with antibiotics. The pulmonologist ordered a chest x-ray which showed something again was in the lung with a CT scan showing a large tumor in the same location as the one where the large lymphoma was just removed. A PET scan showed it was even malignant. The cancer doctor again said that Shirley needed chemo and moreover, said that if Shirley had the chemo as he had originally recommended, she would not have this problem .But my engineering and scientific training told me this wasn't logical. How could a tumor reoccur in the same spot as where just six weeks before one was removed? I researched medical records and couldn't find a single record of any such occurrence. I consulted other doctors including the medical director of Baptist hospital who was a pulmonologist and who said this could be a noninfectious inflammation of the scar tissue created where the tumor was removed six weeks before.

But the cancer doctor and pulmonologist persisted with their strong message "Get Chemo". Fortunately, we had a friend who was director of Rheumatology at the University of Miami School of Medicine and he referred us to the chief of oncology at its Sylvester Cancer Institute. He agreed to work with us with further tests before going into the chemo routine which had almost killed Shirley 8 years before with the breast cancer treatments.

I fired the oncologist and pulmonologist and we went to U of M's Sylvester Cancer Clinic. We decided to run tests over the next several months to determine what Shirley had and these tests included a bronchoscope going all the way into the lungs and a core needle biopsy taking a sample of tissue where the tumor was supposed to be.

Neither of these were conclusive but Shirley's cough started to improve with a steroidal inhalant and the next CT scan in three months showed a reduced mass. We continued monitoring Shirley's lung situation over the following year with CT scans every three months and what do you know, There was no tumor, it was a non infectious inflammation and she didn't need the chemo after all. My diagnosis was right. The doctor's diagnosis was wrong. The problem this situation illustrates the difference between "cookbook and patient profile medicine" and patient specific medicine.

The Sylvester oncology chief, himself a nationally noted expert on lymphomas had likened Shirley's problem to looking for weapons of mass destruction in Shirley's lung and not finding them even after "invading" her lung(The Iraq War story). He said he could have sworn she did have another lymphoma but in the end, agreed with the diagnosis I came up with.

Had we followed Shirley's initial cancer doctor's advice to go the chemo route, it likely would have been Shirley's funeral. As of this writing, 2014, seven years later, there is no evidence or symptoms of cancer anywhere in Shirley and we will celebrate her 80th birthday and celebrate our 60th [h] wedding anniversary aboard our favorite cruise leaving December 1, 2014 with our favorite Capt. Panos.

My next foray into the world of medicine happened about 2008 when there was a national debate about the health care system and how to fix that broken system. The government came up with a monster called "Obamacare" which to me was an inefficient and disastrous approach. I concluded that the way to "fix" the system was to dramatically reduce its costs by accelerating the implementation of then already available technology. I developed a system I named "the virtual clinic" which allows doctors and clinics to seamlessly interface with each other connecting with patients regardless of where they may be. This system electronic medical records and allows the patient to communicate with doctors and clinics via the Internet and email.

I sent this to the CEO of Baptist Hospital system of South Florida who arranged a meeting for me with the hospital system's chief medical officer. I was told I was five years ahead of my time. Today, as I write this book, 2014, there is widespread use of the technologies and systems I described in my "Virtual Clinic".

My next "visit" to the medical world happened about 2010 when I started to have an itch on my face and the back of my head. The dermatologist told me it was a symptom of getting old and told me to shampoo my hair more often with Head & Shoulders and prescribed a topical steroid cream.

After about a year of visiting several dermatologists with the condition getting worse, I gave the VA a shot. After all, I am a veteran and was by then into the VA system as a hearing aid patient.

The VA dermatologist took a biopsy of the skin areas with the resulting diagnosis of skin lupus. Treatment required me to take Paquinil which is an antimalarial drug. But, I could not take that drug until my eyes were extensively tested to make sure the drug wouldn't blind me, which could be a side effect. After taking that drug one year with no results, the doctor put me on a high dosage of Prednisone (steroidal drug) which resolved my itch within 24 hours. After a month on this having to stop because taking this drug for too long could kill me, it was replaced by Cellcept which is steroidal replacement drug taken usually to prevent rejection of major organ transplant (kidney, liver, heart, etc). After this didn't work, the VA doc convinced me to try Thalidomide which is the drug that was given expectant mothers for morning sickness but was taken off the market when deformed babies came out. I took this drug for six weeks with bad side effects and the cost of $15,000 for one pill per day(fortunately the VA paid it all).

After all this, I asked the doc if he had given me a correct diagnosis. He set me up as the "Conference Patient" of the month at the next Dermatology medical conference at which I was examined by 20 dermatologists.

Their consensus diagnosis was that I had "Skin Lymphoma" which is a blood cancer of the leukemia family showing up on the skin instead of internal tumors.

Concurrently, I had found Eric Bussear, a specialist of skin diseases who had taken another biopsy which confirmed the Lymphoma condition. The treatment for "B-Cell Skin Lymphoma" was four weekly infusions (chemo) of Rituxan, a single agent extremely expensive($50,000 per four week course) biotherapy drug plus daily topical steroidal creams on face and scalp. I had my second yearly "round" spring of 2014 and now know that I will have to live with this but also know that the itch condition will never go away. Fortunately, this type of cancer, if controlled, is very unlikely to kill me given my age.

My final comment about my medical "training" concerns Shirley's blood pressure problem. She had been on blood pressure meds for many years with the cardiologist just increasing dosage and more meds as the blood pressure became more difficult to control. When Shirley had the lung lymphoma problem in 2007, the U of M pulmonologist told her she was taking too many blood pressure meds and referred her to the U of M blood pressure specialist doctor. She ran some tests and concluded that Shirley has an hyperactive adrenalin gland, prescribed a cheap potassium sparing diuretic (Spironolectone) and that not only controlled Shirley's blood pressure, but let her stop half of the meds she was taking and reduce the dosage of the others.

Given all this medical training, I have been able to help others in their medical problems and even referring them to the right doctors. Therefore, I feel justified in awarding myself an honorary "doctor" degree.

Gunther's view of religion

Do I believe there is a "God"? To answer this question and I will answer it, we need to examine the creation, the structure of the universe and how all that's within it works.

The scientist tells, per the latest theory, that we live in an exploding universe that started with a "bang" expanding indefinitely. This raises the question of what existed where it started, into "what" did the planets, stars, cosmic dust and comets "explode' and what mechanism triggered all this? What is the "universe"? Is it curved per Einstein's definition or is there a parallel universe as some scientists have considered? If we accept the theory of a constantly expanding universe, what does it expand into?

The religious person accepting the words in the Bible believes that "God" created all there is including the universe, planted Adam in the Garden of Eden with "woman" created from Adam's ribs so that Adam would not be alone and that together they could reproduce more like themselves to populate Earth.

But does this mean the "Garden of Eden" was created on our planet Earth and not some other planet somewhere in the universe and that the humans we have become today did not originate on some other planet in another galaxy? Could the human form as we today know possibly have been colonized from a planet in another galaxy? After all, according to astronomers, our planet "Earth" is a typical planet within a typical solar system within a typical galaxy.

Who can say for certainty and with proof that life as we know it, based on biblical theory was created on our planet Earth?

I am 81 years old as of this writing in 2014. This means that the "system" that's my body has functioned with the heart pumping, kidneys cleansing fluids, digestive system processing foods and the bladder and bowels expelling waste and lungs inhaling oxygen driving this entire bodily system.

How was such a complex "living system" created and how is it possible for it to function for 81 years and there are people living beyond 100 years of age?

The human requires food which comes from animals and plants as well as water which makes up over 95% of the body's content. Science explains the evolution of life per the Darwinian theory but how was such a seemingly perfectly harmonious system and process created in the first place?

Is there really a supernatural entity which created this universe of planets, living beings and processes which makes all this function in what seems a perpetual machine? That is the question which I now will answer.

Being the scientist that I am with substantial understanding of the workings of the universe and earthly systems, I acknowledge that there is a force throughout the universe that made all this happen. I reach this conclusion because there is no logical other explanation. I also accept the principle of seeking guidance and from a supernatural being, whatever it may be called, when all else fails. Whether this is called prayer or meditation is not important. What is important is that it becomes a focus of the problem and the means of moving beyond what may seem like an impossible and unsolvable problem.

So yes, I do believe there is a force permeating throughout the universe which in ways we yet do not understand that has given life to the universe and all that exists therein. This acknowledges my belief that here may be a supernatural force throughout the fabric of the universe.

Is this "force" a supernatural "force " which can be called "God"? I don't know. What form would such "God" take? I don't know but most likely in the likeness of a human which allows understanding by people.

The form "such 'God" takes historically has evolved with the intelligence and knowledge level of humans. In the beginning during primitive times, "God" appeared in the form of a rock, the sun or moon which can be physically seen.

As earth became more civilized with people becoming more intelligent, the concept of "God" became more and more a matter of "belief" and "faith" in how prophets interpreted the concept of a supernatural being or force. I also acknowledge that the perception and form of such God may take on the form that evolved on a particular planet and that how an intelligent being looks may vary dramatically from planet to planet and galaxy to galaxy. I also acknowledge the probability that 'Earth" is not the only planet in the entire universe where some form of intelligence exists. Moreover, I believe that the intelligent form we know as "human" may not be the only "form" of intelligence in the universe nor indeed maybe even in our own galaxy known as the Milky Way.

This brings in ""religion" and I will herein share my view on "religion". "Religion" is the interpretation of the universe's supernatural force giving a name such as "God", Allah, Jehovah etc. . Religions have been created by prophets who define the supernatural and how worship of such a God should be practiced. Prophets have written books prescribing the details of these variant interpretations of "God" and means of worshipping. The book giving the Judeo Christian version of belief originating from Abraham is called "The Bible". The Islamic form taking off from the Abrahamic belief was created by Muhammad and is called the "Koran". Yet another variant of the Judeo Christian religion was created by Joseph Smith and is called "the Book of Mormon". The Christian religion takes off from the Bible's "Old Testament" with the coming of Jesus Christ who Christians believe is the Son of God which creates and adds the New Testament to the Bible.

While the Jewish religion believes that the Messiah is yet to come, the Christians believe that Jesus Christ is the Messiah who died and who will again come someday. Then, there are many variants of each of these religions.

It is my view that "Religion" since its very beginning, instead of helping to make this world a better one, has evolved as the most destructive and deadly force in the history of mankind.

The basis of this destructive characteristic is that each religion and variants thereof believes that it's belief and version of religion is the only true belief and any person not believing theirs should either convert to their true belief or be killed or sent to hell.

Examples of religious based destruction go all the way back to biblical days when constant wars existed between the Jews and others such as the Assyrians, Romans and Greeks. Going forward in history we recall the Crusades. Then, bands of Christians roamed from the Brit Isles south through Europe killing nonbelievers along the way all the way to Jerusalem. There the Crusaders killed the Muslims and occupied the holy city until they were themselves thrown out by Saladin who in the name of the Muslim God, Allah evicted the Christians and drove them back to Northern Europe. Then we come to the Spanish Inquisition when the Pope encouraged Spanish Queen Isabella to cleanse the Iberian Peninsula of the Jews forcing them to convert, flee or be killed.

Not well known was the Thirty Year War 1618-1648 when Swedish peasants revolted to throw out the Catholics who had it all while the peasants were starving. The catalyst for this "war" was the Reformation of Martin Luther who started the Protestant religion which believed that a person did not need a priest as an intermediary praying to God. But the Swedes weren't satisfied by throwing out the Catholics from Sweden. They invaded Germany and swept east through Russia reaching all the way to Moscow. After 30 years of hell with people being killed over religion, the Swedes were finally conquered by one brutal Russian winter.

Now, lets move to current times. In the 1800's, Jews were persecuted with many killed during the pogroms of eastern Europe including Ukraine and Poland. This was followed by Hitler and his Nazi regime cleansing Europe of 75% of all its Jews including the killing of over 6 million Jews and displacing millions more(including myself personally) in the Holocaust.

More recently, we witnessed the brutal killings between Protestants and Catholics in Northern Ireland followed by the religious based ethnic cleansing in the Balkans.

My Life – Global Society Rising

Today, 2014, we see the on again war between Israel, a Jewish state and the Palestinians of Gaza. And the rise of the ISIS Caliphate(Islamic State of Iraq and Syria) consisting of radical Sunni Muslims marauding throughout the Syria and Iraq killing their Shia Muslim brothers because they are on the wrong side of the Islamic faith.

We see fanatics on all sides using religion as their weapon for carrying out their own agenda. Fanatical Christians bomb abortion clinics and murder their doctors claiming the doctors are baby killers. We saw the assassination of Yitzhak Rabin, the Israeli Prime Minister, by a radical Jew of an ultra orthodox group because Rabin was trying to make peace with Egypt and the ultra orthodox Jews don't believe in a secular State of Israel. Islamic fanatics brain wash their teenagers into becoming suicide bombers so they can go to their heaven and be caressed by young virgins. It is commonplace for a Christian to tell a friend that he is not a true believer and a Christian because, according to his belief, if he has not said a certain prayer aloud confessing sins, he will go to hell.

My view of religious belief is about love for fellow man, forgiveness of sins and people helping one another. I believe that the supernatural force of the universe, be it called God, Allah, Jehovah etc., gave us at birth the means of living a good and productive life. This is a brain to think with, hands to work with and feet to walk with.

If we are to pray to "God", we should pray for the wisdom to use these faculties better. Unfortunately and in reality, this fundamental belief common to all major religions has been hijacked by the fanatics in all religions who use religion for political and economic self interests. That makes religion as widely practiced today destructive rather than constructive.

Yes, I do mention economic self interests because religion has become the biggest business in history. The bible is the biggest selling book, there is a church, synagogue or mosque nearly on every corner each with its own pastor, rabbi or imman sucking money from their congregants in the name of their God. We see televangelists clad in heavenly robes preaching from glass walled castles raking in $$$ billions of donations from round the world. While many congregations do much good, as a whole, they suck out enormous capital from the economy. Shirley & I once entered a cathedral in Lima Peru, where beggars on its front door steps asked for pennies for food while as we entered there stood a two ton statue made of solid gold and silver.

What religion do I believe in? None that exists. I believe that we all should focus more on what all these religions have in common far more than how they differ. If the best of all major religions could be combined into a single religion, that would be really great. But that's not realistic. But I do believe that if all religions just followed the "Ten Commandments" and practiced the teaching of Jesus and Rabbi Akiva that being 'Love thy neighbor as thyself" , that would be a great start. I also believe that each religion should be tolerant of the others. Who is to say what's the best way to practicea belief ?

One illustration of how to practice what I believe is the right way occurred on a cruise. We were having early morning coffee on the aft deck of a large cruise ship. Shirley saw a short bearded man sitting at the next table reading a small bible with an accent. She asked the man 'Where are you from?" He answered "Jerusalem". Shirley thinking he might be a rabbi from Israel said "that's nice…you are from Israel." He then said, " Yes, but I am from East Jerusalem and was raised in Amman, Jordan. I am a Palestinian Arab and the book I am reading is the Koran." Shortly thereafter, his wife arrived. A blond lady from Germany.

We became friends on the cruise and this friendship has lasted for years. A Palestinian Arab, a German woman, a Jewish holocaust survivor from Germany and a Jewish daughter of Polish immigrants.

One year, he insisted on us visiting them in Toronto and we spent four days as his house guests. At one breakfast, sitting around the table were the four of us plus his other guest for breakfast, a visiting Islamic scholar from Medina, Saudi Arabia. Instead of killing each other because of our radically different beliefs and cultures, we all had friendly discussions about the Arab –West conflicts, religious differences and world events. This to me is what I believe is how people should behave. Talking together instead of killing each other. This is what I believe true brotherly love and tolerance is about and that is what today's religions are mostly without.

Then, there is politics. I strongly believe that personal religious beliefs have no place in government. A religious based government is a "theocracy" . The Islamic form of this is called 'Caliphate" which is precisely what the ISIS (Islamic Government of Iraq and Syria) has become. The head of this "government" is called the "Caliph" who in common language is their dictator who in the name of "Islam" orders its disciples to kill anyone not believing and practicing its specific and narrowly defined form of Sunni Islam.

What religious congregations have we belonged to? Shirley & I were both born to Jewish parents and therefore are definitely Jewish. When I was sent to Sweden after my family was persecuted and killed by the Nazis because they were Jewish, I lived with a deeply religious Christian farming family. Along with the family, I went to their Lutheran church and also to their weekly prayer meetings as they were Pentecostal believers. My foster parents taught me the difference between good and bad, important values in life and the importance of believing in 'something". This remained with me always.

After five years living with my Christian foster family, I was sent to a Jewish orphanage where there was no religion that I can recall. Then on to an extremely orthodox Jewish family in Stockholm where the focus of life was observing strict adherence to kosher dietary rules, not riding cars or street cars on the Sabbath and learning Hebrew preparing for the Bar Mitzvah ceremony.

Gunther Karger

When I lived with my next foster family in the U.S. for 4 years, they were super reformed going to a reform Jewish temple. After they had "thrown me out" at age 17 and later when telling them I would be marrying Shirley whose family was orthodox Jewish, they said that orthodox Jews are low class people and wouldn't attend my wedding.

After we were married, Shirley & I always belonged to a Jewish reform temple, sent our sons to Sunday school and practiced the basics of the Jewish religion. Then, when it became too expensive for us to remain in the temple we had belonged to for ten years, we tried a few others. I kept looking for the kind of people and beliefs I had experienced living with my Christian Swedish family who believed more in the fundamentals of being "good" than how much money is contributed, what kind of car one drives or the size of the house.

We found this in a Messianic Jewish temple in Ft. Lauderdale, Florida . This temple believed the principle of combining the Christian faith with Jewish traditions with the people worshipping the art of doing good more than how much money one donates. We left this "temple" after ten years because it gravitated more toward being too fanatical as the American political scene became involved too much with right wing beliefs. We returned to a traditional Jewish congregation but left when we moved to Homestead. We could have remained but even that temple was far too much oriented to money things and nearly no concern for fellow members.

When we moved to Homestead, we discovered a small non denominational church where the pastor could become a friend and the people seemed sincerely interested in each other as a "person".

When the congregation fell on less than good financial footing and needed to reduce costs, I helped arrange the church to meet in the available empty space in the local Jewish temple where they hold services and social functions. This illustrates what I believe is good religion. People of different faiths respecting their differences but working together for the common good.

However, when the pastor decided to close his church rather than take less In salary to continue serving his flock, we rejoined the "Temple of Life" otherwise known as the "church of the street". This became yet another illustration how people proclaiming to spread the "word of their God" serve themselves instead of shepherding their flock.

I believe there are entirely too many religions and places of worships and that one day, there will be just a few left as either they have come to their senses, gone bankrupt or killed each other off.

My Family

We have two sons, Herbert born in Baton Rouge, Louisiana March 22, 1958, just three months before my graduation from LSU. Herb was named after my Father. Our second son, Kenneth was born 15 months later June 29, 1959 just after we moved to New Jersey. Ken was named after my astronomy professor reflecting my love for space and science. Shirley & I were married December 5, 1954 in New Orleans at a huge Jewish wedding and celebrate our 60th wedding anniversary as this book is released aboard our anniversary cruise.

Given my Holocaust background losing my entire family and somehow ingrained belief that it is the husband's responsibility to take care of his family including wife and children, that became a priority in all that we did. Shirley's life's goal and dream was to have children, attend their weddings, be friends with their extended families, help them when they had their own children, attend the Bar Mitzvah or Bas Mitzvah of our grand children and see them grow up eventually with their own families.

While our sons were growing up all the way through high school, Shirley dedicated herself to our family, stayed at home making it nice for everyone sacrificing her own professional career which given her personality and interests could have been sales or teaching. She did have part time jobs at JC Penney's, gift stores and did a lot of market research surveys, substitute teaching which helped with the family income.

We always had a nice house and made sure our sons had all that they needed and we could afford. Wherever we lived, we joined a Jewish temple where Herb & Ken went to Sunday school and eventually had their Bar Mitzvahs with a big party and all family members invited.

The boys became interested in magic and became magicians. I bought them lots of magic tricks and they put on magic shows for many years at birthday parties and even were on a TV show, at hotel functions and several conventions. Shirley made a deal with the local Howard Johnson's restaurant for the boys to put on their show at birthday parties and she drove them to the shows.

Shirley became the Cub Scout den mother taking care of our sons and their friends at scouting events. We sent them several summers to Boy Scout Camp and took them with one some of our vacations.

We wanted to teach the boys responsibility of earning their own money and Herb was a Fuller Brush salesman and both worked for an avocado picker.

To give them a bridge to my own past and family which had been lost in the Holocaust, we took them on a trip to Sweden where I had lived and they spent several summers on the Gustafson farm with my foster family and even learned a little Swedish. The Jewish Federation had a High School in Israel program in which students as a group went to a six week school in Israel. We sent our sons to this school at separate times so they would learn about their Jewish heritage and world history first hand.

To foster a "Father – Son" "relationship, I took each son on separate trips, this being made possible by cheap air fares as I worked for Eastern Airlines. I took Herb to San Francisco and Ken to Guatemala. When Ken graduated High School, we took him on a cruise and sent him on a 3 week trip on European railroads when he graduate college.

All was well with our family until Herb became interested in guitar music at about 15 and wanted to join the school rock band. We gave in and unfortunately got him a guitar. He gravitated toward friends who did not have good habits.. He attended Webber College, a small private college in midstate Florida. He did have some health problems but managed to graduate. All this took a toll on us emotionally and financially. We helped him get a good job with Ryder system after graduation.

He was a hard worker when he worked but didn't always work at jobs with much future. Eventually, he did get married fortunately to a girl with a nice and well to do father who picked up where we left off.

Ken on the other hand maintained good habits, attended and graduated Florida State University and even got a masters degree. I had visions of us working together in real estate after my own retirement so together, we both attended Real Estate school and got our individual broker licenses. When Ken graduated Florida State, I helped him get a job with the real estate dept. of a bank and on his own he got a job with the biggest commercial real estate company in Miami. Unfortunately, none of them worked out well and after a period of no work, hurricane Andrew came to save him. He got a job with the Government SBA disaster program which lasted ten years.

When the Miami job ended, he got transferred to the SBA in New Orleans but didn't like it and walked off the job coming home just as Shirley was undergoing her cancer and chemo. Fortunately, we had the condo we had bought years before so we let him move into it. I was able to provide a retirement program giving him sufficient retirement income. Ken never married but has a long time Jewish girlfriend.

Our Family

This year, in 2014, as we celebrate our 60th anniversary we live in a great retirement community in a lovely house just for the two of us. We will end our lives by focusing on each other knowing that beyond ourselves and our sons, there is no extension into future generation. When our "day" comes, we will know that our legacy lives on by our deeds and the good we were able to contribute to society. We then can rest easy knowing we did the best we could.

While we have a few good friends, our dream of having grand children is unfulfilled and we know that our family won't be extended beyond us. Shirley has over the years "collected" many "grand children" from all around the world by giving them presents, reading to them and doing good in the community. The toughest days for us, especially Shirley, is during holidays when she sees so many other people celebrating with their families and we have just the two of us.

The picture below is Shirley reading to one of her street classes, children of migrant workers she collects at a launderette next to the Homestead Goodwill store. This picture tells much about Shirley and that we go on into our sunset years making the best of what we have and we had a lot to be thankful for. We have the two of us, a nice home, a few good friends and still go on our annual cruises and a few other trips.

Book Two

Global Society Rising

Book One tells the story of my life in context of my experience which is unusually broad and deep. This gives me an unusual understanding and an ability to comprehend complex and diverse things. Most importantly, this ability has provided me the gift of seeing into the future and describe what It very likely will become.

Book 2 looks at our society as it has evolved over recent years and projects it to what it most likely will become over the next 20 years unless radical changes in how we manage ourselves are made. This projection is made on the basis of momentum, inertia and Psycho Historic Morphology (PHM) which I will introduce in the following chapter.

Since 9/11, we have seen a paradoxial world evolving. **On the negative side**, we have seen the emergence of these drivers of destruction:

- Rise of fanaticism
- Equalization of society in the USA
- Destructive politics
- Dark side of Political correctness
- Collapsing economy
- Obamacare – wrong turn toward healthcare
- Rising domestic violence
- Decline in technology leadership

On the positive side, we see:

- Acceleration of technology
- Globalization
- Increasing global concern about the environment
- Awakening to a new world by under developed nations
- Rising economies of under developed regions

I will address these issues in Book 2 drawing from my unique and broad personal experience given in book I. Then, I will describe the new world as I see evolving over the span of 20 years or said in another way, the next generation.

It is my sincere hope that this book, most likely my final, will share lessons that should have been learned from the past and guidance for the future. I hope this will help you, as an individual, to better plan your own life and you, as a business leader, better guide your company. While most people are focused on "today" and the very near term, I focus on the long term and yes, even the very long term beyond the remaining life spans of many of us.

There is much hope for our world going forward but also, much change lies ahead. What counts is that we as individuals and business leaders alike, learn the lessons of history. Those who do will survive and maybe even prosper. But those who don't will fall by the wayside.

It's most important for us to learn and embed into our ingrained thinking that change is not only inevitable but is accelerating. Those who don't learn this and try to move back to old times are doomed to fail. Why? Because those who try to recover the past fail to heed the most basic principle of the universe: The hands of the clock move clockwise forward to the right. If we try to reverse this, the clock will break as will our lives.

While you may not agree with my assessment of the world as I see it nor the world I see ahead, I hope this book at least gives you a new perspective.

Gunther - A futurist

One of the most important events in "My Life" was the introduction to science fiction. Why? Because that, in addition to having to find ways overcoming insurmountable obstacles to life gave me the vision of believing that nearly all things are possible. The experience of "My Life" told me that there always is a way to "get through today's problem", find a solution and somehow manage to see yet another "tomorrow". My very presence today is proof of this principle.

Science fiction also taught me that there is a future "beyond just tomorrow" which is "hope" that drives me to always focus on the future ranging from the "Day after tomorrow" to beyond my own lifetime. If I were asked to define the person I have become, I would be remembered as a "Futurist".

The sum of my experience throughout "My Life" gave me direct and very personal insight into an unusual diversity of complex situations stretching from local "here today" to global and even to a limited way, space. But it was not the individual experiences that was to become the most significant factor leading me to better understand life and the world as it is. It is the combined aggregate and synergy of all the very diverse situations I experienced.

What if any was the single most significant factor that made it possible for me to conceive the "total systems approach" to problem solving and the creation of new ideas?

While science fiction was important, it was the concept created by Dr. Isaac Asimov, in his "Foundation" series of books. Dr. Asimov(Yudovich Ozimov, born 1920) who was Professor of Biochemistry at Boston University and one of the greatest, if not the greatest, science fiction writer of all times. In my view, Asimov and his contemporaries Robert Heinlein and Arthur C. Clarke defined science fiction and carried on what Jules Verne created in the previous century. These authors had the vision of what actual science would become years later.

I learned a great deal from these authors which enabled me to conceive some of the systems in my actual work assignments over the years

Asimov's "Foundation" series of books introduced a new science he called "Psychohistory" in which he combined history, mathematics and psychology into a tool wherein it became possible not only to predict the future, but also to influence on what the future would become". The setting of this "Foundation" series was in a futuristic galactic empire about 25,000 years into the future revolving around a young college mathematics professor who had been discovered by the emperor. The Emperor assigned this professor, Hari Seldon, the job of refining his theories so the emperor could stop the erosion of his crumbling empire. The emperor also decreed that a "Foundation" be established to gather the best brains in the galaxy to develop this science as far as possible.

While at the ICS team, and assigned to create a system to work after 100 nuclear bombs had destroyed the U.S. (see prior chapters), I discovered another new approach to systems design called 'Morphological Creativity" by Dr. Myron Allen, then a consultant in Physics and Industrial Psychology. Dr. Allen believed he found a new approach to releasing hidden brain power by creating a three dimensional system of developing very large complex systems and successfully used them at Hughes Aircraft, Douglas Aircraft and Aerojet General during the early sixties. In a sense, the ICS team I addressed in the prior chapter was the 20th century version of the emperor's foundation as created by Asimov.

Psychohistoric Morphology (PHM)

I combined Dr. Allen's "Morphology" and Dr. Asimov's "Psychohistory" to create "Psychohistoric Morphology" or "PHM" to create the "post doomsday recovery system" I described in the ICS chapters and have used this technique in developing a number of systems over the years.

The latest application resulted from the recent massive financial meltdown of 2007-2012. I structured and developed a concept for a massive data warehouse combining modified intelligence software for early detection in financial and securities fraud. I have reason to believe that my concept formed the basis of what is being implemented by federal regulators.

PHM uses a multi dimensional model combining Asimov's and Allen's systems so that simple answers can be found for complex problems and requirements. The dimensions of this model are:

- Requirements, problem to be solved
- Technology resources available
- Financial resources to implement
- Societal and political constraints
- Environmental constraints and resolutions
- Uncontrollable factors
- Time constraints
- Human behavior

The use of this model is actually simple. Here is how it's done.

- Define the problem in detail
- Identify all potential resources to solve the problem
- Identify the constraints while stretching the constraints beyond their known limits.
- Factor in a deep understanding of human behavior
- Construct a multidimensional matrix to identify where the problem intersects with solution and select the best.

So what's the catch? This system must be used by a person with specific and very diverse knowledge of scientific principles, availability of systems which could be used , deep understanding of global societies, human behavior and lastly, economic and political matters. Alternatively, the "single person" can be augmented by people with significant wide experience along with appropriate computer resources which can be accessed for matrix match capability.

I have herein gone into significant technical detail describing PHM because I used this radically new system to predict the Global Society that's in the early stages of evolving. As you read on, keep in mind the unique and very diverse experience I personally draw from. That's what gives me the ability to do this with reasonable accuracy. I also recognize that the accuracy of my predictions will be measured beyond my life time.

There are some who from this "dissertation" might assume I am a learned PhD having done much theoretical study at universities. No, my formal university degree is "Electrical Engineer" plus many specialized courses in multiple technologies, economics,investments, psychology and licensure qualification.

Since no university awarded me a PhD, I will award myself the degree of "PhD" of "The application of life experiences and survival" and I indeed declare this is earned rather than "honorary". The "University" awarding me this distinction is "The Global University of Experience". What distinguishes me from the traditional PhD awardee is that instead of spending years in classrooms learning and writing dissertations, I spent a lifetime "experiencing and doing it".

So where is my "Doctorate Dissertation"? Why it's right here. It's this book which tells what I actually experienced and did. You are reading it and it's issued by **" Global University of Experience".**

Decline of U.S. World Influence

Since its founding in 1776, America as the United States became known, steadily rose in its position as a bastion of leadership in world affairs. The synergy of the diverse people seeking economic opportunity, fleeing political oppression and religious freedom all came together to form the new and exceptionally strong country it became.

America's strength came from diverse people working together toward common goals to maintain the freedoms and opportunity gained. Regardless of where they came from, they learned a common language which was English so they could communicate among themselves and learned to bridge their cultural differences so they could become friends and effectively work together. Despite still bringing along some weaknesses such as slavery of black people and prejudices against some minorities such as the Jews, the country grew stronger and gained world influence..

Substantial progress was made by eliminating slavery and reducing prejudices against minorities over the years gave minorities greater opportunities and freedom to express themselves which added to America's strength. By the early 19th Century, America became a world leading power joining the UK and Russia in defeating Germany in WW I.

America had been drawn into that war triggered by German U-boats (submarines) attacking American ships and Germany offering to help Mexico to start a war against America. America once again joined UK and Russia to defeat Germany and Japan in WW II. These wars led to America's rise as a super power resulting from it gaining leadership in technology, making new and better arms, airplanes and manufacturing and especially the development of the atomic bomb and space rockets. After WW II ended, America became a leader in helping Europe including Russia to reconstruct itself which contributed to America's rise in world trade.

Although Russia (then called Soviet Union) was the first to launch a man into space, America soon caught up this lead and far exceeded it in most forms of military and civilian technologies. The Moon project of the Sixties became a major contributor to America's world leadership in technology and as a super power.

Unfortunately, as has happened to every world super power going all the way back to ancient empires like Alexander the Great who conquered the world for Greece by age 30, the Roman empire, Napoleon, Brits and every empire that tries to conquer the world, America didn't learn from this history. It became the self appointed world leader against communism starting in Korea against the North Koreans empowered by communist China and continued this in Vietnam after the French tried and failed.

The 9/11 attack in 2001 triggered the next phase of America extending itself as influencer of the kind of government it felt was the best for other cultures and peoples. Instead of focusing on dealing with the terrorists, George Bush decided to invade Iraq to overthrow its dictator. Obama succeeding Bush did the same in Afghanistan trying to bring America's form of democracy to a country founded on rule bywar lords driven by an economy based on opium (heroin) production.

Neither president had learned the clear lessons of history which teaches that trying to enforce one's own form of government on peoples of other cultures has never worked. Worse still, all countries or empires which have tried this, eventually weakened and collapsed.

This is what is today happening in America or properly called The United States of America. I make the transition from "America" to the United States because today, in 2014, the name "America" no longer stands for what it once did..

The following several chapters give the basic drivers for this decline"

- Rise of fanaticism
- Equalization of society in the USA
- Destructive politics
- Dark side of Political correctness
- Collapsing economy
- Obamacare – wrong turn in healthcare
- Rising domestic violence
- Decline in technology leadership
- Impact of immigration policy

While this decline has been allowed to progress quite far, there fortunately is time to arrest and reverse it. Example of a prediction of doom occurred in 1985 when I issued a forecast for Eastern Airlines top leadership that unless it changed its corporate strategy, it would fail(see previous chapter on the collapse of Eastern Airlines). Instead of heeding the prediction which included specific ways to avoid the collapse, I was fired. It was a message no one wanted to hear. Today, few people have even heard of Eastern Airlines which pioneered aviation and at one time was one of the largest airlines in the world.

To reverse the trend which still is in place as of the time this book is written (2014), the U.S. must find a new kind of leadership. In particular, leaders who must know and learn the lessons of history.

The final chapter in this book will tell what likely will happen in the U.S.(once called America) by the year 2035 assuming that the right kind of new leaders will not emerge with the destructive trends today in place continuing.

Gunther Karger

Rise of Global Fanaticism

What is "fanaticism?" The dictionary says "*Excessive enthusiasm inspired by religious belief*". I take this to the bottomline which is "*My way is ordained by God and our differences are irreconcilable*". Taken to extreme, this leads to "*You either adopt my belief and ways of worshipping this belief or I will kill you*".

A mother killed her five children in the fanatical belief that "God" told her to do so. Paul Hill, the religious fundamentalist believed that abortion is murder so strongly than he converted his religious belief into earthly law and shot an abortion doctor who violated "his law" as he believed was ordained by God.

The ultra orthodox Jewish religious zealot shot and killed Israel's Prime Minister Rabin because he was negotiating peace with Egypt but believed that the State of Israel should be ruled by God instead of by "Man". The Catholic rulers of Spain forced anyone not of Catholic faith to convert to it or be killed as a nonbeliever. In 2014, hordes calling themselves ISIS (Islamic State of Iraq and Syria) rampaged throughout the Mideast killing thousands of people who did not convert to their specific brand of Sunni Muslim faith including women, children and ravaged entire villages.

Fanaticism invaded the American political scene with its rise triggered by the fanatical "9/11" terrorist attack destroying the New York World Trade Center killing over 3,000 people. This historic event caused fanaticism about "You are either with us or against us" with this belief morphing from the personal level to the halls of Washington.

This led to the increased politicization of the abortion issue or better put, "Right to Life vs Right to Choice" centered on when life begins before birth and its relation to religious belief. This further led to the increasingly unbending beliefs on both sides and the taking of irreconcilable sides by the far right and far left with anyone in the middle becoming nearly irrelevant.

Eventually, this led to paralysis in the Congress which could not even pass a budget eventually leading to a government shutdown. The paralysis got so bad that the president had to resort to executive orders to just keep some essential parts of government going.

Fanaticism has always been part of the fabric of civilization since the beginning of time when living things including humans were sacrificed to gain salvation by some particular God. Excessive fanaticism by its very nature has led to political and national chaos where someone strong enough has emerged to restore order by exerting military force.

Example of the necessity of using force to keep order was the rule of Saddam Hussein, Iraqi dictator who kept order in Iraq by keeping two basic religious antagonist groups from killing each other by oppressing one side with military force. When he was deposed by the U.S. in the interest of "freeing the oppressed bringing democracy", chaos erupted eventually leading to the collapse of Iraq and the return of U.S. to prevent Iraq being over run by the ISIS fanatical hordes of 2014.

Another example was Egypt when Mubarak, an army colonel took over the government and maintained that order for a generation via a dictatorial regime. He was overthrown by the people demonstrating freedom and who installed a new president(Morsi). Instead of doing what the people elected him to do, Morsi tried to reinstall his own brand of Islamic belief supported by the mostly radical Muslim Brotherhood. Then, just a year later, Egypt was saved by Gen. Sisi, the Army Chief by him overthrowing Morsi in the interest of again saving Egypt from the religious fanatics. All this in the course of fanatical waves.

History tells us that fanaticism always leads to political and national chaos causing loss of lives and destroying countries. It appears that America's leaders the post 9/11 era either never learned the lessons of history or believed their particular belief would overcome the fanatics.

What these people didn't realize is that they themselves were creating their own form of fanaticism destined to failure, eventual chaos and the necessity for someone to "save" the country from itself.

It is my view, based on history, that the United States is getting dangerously close to the edge of disaster unless its leaders back away from their religiously motivated unbending beliefs (fanaticism) and find that "common ground" which is always "there" if looked for. The inflexibility in Washington has already found its way into local communities where friends and neighbors become bitter enemies solely because of opposite religious driven secular principles. This "craze" even led to the idea that everyone should have the right to bear guns which led to an epidemic of shootings and even mass killings in schools and theaters.

Unless leaders and individuals start realizing that the common ground to all major religions is found in the Ten Commandments, military officers will eventually decide to form a group to "save' the country from itself. They would install a very different kind of government where the people will have a lot less freedom. Make sure you read my final chapters which tell how this could easily unfold into reality during the current generation.

Destructive trends in the U.S.

9/11 started a trend of emerging forces increasingly contributing to the U.S. declining world standing. This included a number of factors I will address in the following chapters:

- Destructive politics
- Equalization of American society
- Dark side of political correctness
- Collapsing economy
- Obamacare – wrong turn in health care
- Rising domestic violence
- Declining world technology leadership
- Impact of failed immigration policy

Destructive Politics

The country is in trouble when candidates for office focus more to find dirt on their opponents than ways to resolve critical issues. When this level of political warfare is reached, real problems aren't resolved and indeed get worse. This reached critical levels with the transition of government from George W. Bush to Barak Obama in 2008. This got so bad in Washington that Congress failed to pass an operating budget for two years leading the nation into default triggering shutdown of government agencies which were forced to lay off government workers. The media called it "Paralysis in Washington" and a national disgrace. Who was responsible for this? The Congress and the President by focusing on opposing ideologies rather than the business of operating the massive government of the U.S. A. .

An example of this government paralysis and what I call federal mismanagement was the U.S Immigration and border patrol problem. Instead of focusing on how to deal with the 11 million undocumented (illegal) aliens already in the country and securing the borders, congress and the president used this as a political football. The situation got so bad in border states that Arizona bordering Mexico passed its own immigration laws to deal with its own security. Tragically, instead of this becoming a wakeup call for the federal government to deal nationally with this problem, the government objected, declared the Arizona law illegal and took the matter to the Supreme Court and nothing happened to solve the problem.

Political warfare wasn't restricted to Washington. In 2014, a Texas city prosecutor was arrested for drunk driving and the governor asked her to step down until she had recovered from her problem. She refused and the governor vetoed funding for one of the programs administered by that prosecutor.

In retaliation, the prosecutor convened a grand jury charging the governor of criminal behavior and actually indicted him.

The TV showed the governor being arrested. By 2014, this political divide had got so pervasive into the fabric of America that it had arrived to the local scene. During the election campaign for Miami Dade county commissioner, the candidate campaigning against the incumbent commissioner sent out flyers accusing her opponent of poisoning children with arsenic and giving herself a raise. These, being outright lies, became political party line campaign issues obscuring the real business of running one of the largest metropolitan governments in the country. The lies prevailed in the election with the incumbent losing.

The divide between liberals and conservatives accelerated focused on gun control while massacres were seen in theatres, schools and other public places. In one instance, a teenager used an assault gun in school to kill a dozen students and a teacher.

The controlling factor in gun control is the super strong and politically controlling National Rifle Association (NRA) whose business it is to make it easy for its industry sponsors to sell weapons and right wing members to use them without restrictions. The gun control issue comes up in Washington in a public outcry every time there is a massacre using guns but after some debate, proposals to deal with it fade away until the next massacre. The "Right to bear Arms" provision in the constitution has become the unbending dividing line between the political parties and gradually over time, makes enemies of friends and neighbors.

Meanwhile, Washington remained in paralysis creating near national chaos .Failure to address real problems such as massive uncontrolled border crossings by aliens, bridges breaking killing people in cars tumbling into rivers because the federal highway administration doesn't have the money to repair bridges, tunnels and Interstate highways all led to a high level of distrust and disgust of the federal government.

This political paralysis and divide eventually caused rising civil unrest by people not trusting their government. More and more people stopped paying taxes in protest.

The number of armed militias accelerated with angry people many of whom were ex military well equipped with all kinds of military gear and weapons. This could risk the country bringing itself to a state of revolution.

As of the writing of this book which is fall of 2014, the political divide in Washington is as strong as ever further expanding to state and local political levels.

Equalization of Society

The lowest common denominator (LCD) is a mathematical expression defining the lowest common level whole numbers can be divided down to. Applying this to society, the LCD becomes the equalizer of societal levels and if taking this principle to extreme, there will result a single society wherein all differences have been removed.

The ultimate of this principle would lead to a society where all assets have been distributed to all inhabitants of that society such that everyone is equal in wealth(or poverty) with equal rights to whatever may be left as a result of this equalization process. In the highly unlikely and for sure, undesirable realization of such societal equalization process, any and all incentives for individuals and business to excel will have become neutralized or saying this in another way, destroyed. The motivation to do better will have been lost.

This applies to individuals who have lost opportunity to get ahead, business owners the incentive to make more money by working harder while exposing the winners to be taxed the fruits of doing better.

Socialist countries ruled by communist regimes try to achieve societal equalization by nationalizing private companies and assets. Examples of this are the former Soviet Union, Cuba under Castro, Venezuela under Chavez and his successor and China under Mao Tse Tung who led its communist revolution against the capitalist Chiang Kai Check.

A different version of this is illustrated by the various Arab kingdoms or sometimes called Sheikhdoms where the ruling family owns everything and distributes the means of making a living to its extended family members with the rest having nearly nothing. The same principle applies to Central Asia warlords who rule smaller regions where the warlord's family owns nearly everything with the rest relying on them for a basic living. This is similar to Middle Age times when the land baron owned everything with the serfs being their kept servants.

Societal equalization first surfaced in the industrialized world with the rise of unions which demanded and received better for its members from their employees. Unionization resulted from excessive greed of the industrialists who in effect were "industrial Barons" compared to the middle age land barons. The unions were needed to force some economic equalization because without a growing population having the means of buying products and services, national economic growth becomes stifled which is good for no one. However, over the years, unions became too strong taking their power over workers to excess eventually exerting enormous influence over industry, business and government.

In the United States, the Great Depression triggered the creation of social economic distribution systems such as Social Security which provided some financial security for the elders and work for the massively unemployed force via the public works program. This helped many people and the country to dig out of a terrible economic crisis and was a good thing. World War II then accelerated the economic recovery but we need to remember that also were created public works programs such as the Interstate Highway project after the War. This was good for the country while also giving people job and business opportunities.

Then came 9/11 which triggered a potential national disaster still is in progress as this book is written in 2014. President George W. Bush handed us the "**You are either with us or against us**" policy which became extremely divisive at all levels of the country. It led to a paranoia centered in the White House against terrorists to the point of even starting a war which later turned out not justified given the reason for it being launched. This was the unjustified Iraq war which followed the attack against Afghanistan which initially was justified. These wars and situations they eventually created led to the U.S. economic collapse and the ascendancy Barack Obama, a black president as a protest vote against President Bush's Republican party.

With President Obama came a policy focused on a shift toward very socialistic and liberal policies. The focus on these policies was social equalization taken to a level never before seen in the U.S. The first focus was the introduction of Obamacare as the means of providing health insurance to all uninsured. This backfired by pitting the Republicans against the Democrats and it didn't work out well during its first years.

Further socially equalizing policies became the focus on absolute equal rights for gays including issuing a presidential support of same sex marriage and further equalization between minorities. While I am not endorsing or opposing such policies, they added to the divisive state between Republicans and Democrats leading to legislative paralysis in Congress. For several years, nearly nothing was done even to the point of failing to agree to a budget triggering a federal government shut down and the downgrade of U.S. Government Bonds in world financial markets.

The socially equalizing policies were extended to the Mideast and Central Asia encouraging its people to rise up to gain freedom and democracy. This led to the Arab Spring which by 2014 created the emergence of the Islamic State, by the worst terrorists the world has ever seen, the collapse of Iraq and chaos in Syria. This emboldened the Hamas, arch enemies of Israel to attack Israel with thousands of rockets and terrorist tunnels far into the Israeli border all of which led to the destruction of Gaza which was the home of over 1.5 million Palestinians.

Yes, freedom and equal rights for all is critically important. However, leaders must be mindful of history, the nature of diverse people and recognize that freedom must be controlled and may be different for diverse cultures. Not recognizing this can lead to chaos and that's where the world was heading in 2014 as this book was written.

Where does this eventually lead? The answer in my view will be given in the final section of this book. It appears to be a certainty however, that the world is headed for further chaos unless there is an awakening and change in national policies. Unless world leaders come to grips with this problem, in just a few years, maybe less than ten years, the people will have less freedom than today as military leaders emerge in the U.S. to save it from itself.

Dark side of Political Correctness

Although "*political correctness*" is related to *"Equalization of Society"*, it is a very important part of the destructive trend the country has faced and unfortunately, continues to face.

Being afraid of insulting the "other" has become part of the destructive process equalizing society to the lowest common dominator where theoretically all of us are equal.

The reality and stark fact is that all of us are not equal nor the same. The way we look at others determines how we perceive others to be and that's reality. Reality is to see each other for "who" and "what" we are and most importantly, respect each other for our differences. This reality gets lost in the current ongoing process of " societal equalization". Social equalization disrespects inherent differences instead of respecting inherent differences. Indeed, social equalization removes the individual right to be different which destroys personal incentives.

It no longer is politically correct to call a person with black skin "black". Today, such a person is "African American".. But what if the person you refer to is a black African from Cape Town in South Africa ? What if the person is a black aborigine from Australia or a person with dark skin from Jamaica? How about the son of an African tribal chief living in London visiting New York. Would you call him " African American"? If a person in this category has to be labeled as to ethnicity, why not label that person in a way common to all which simply is "black"? Best of all would be to not label anyone for anything and relating to all based on "who" they are rather than "what" they are?

Gunther Karger

Language is another problem which severely is increasingly divisive and destructive. It has become "politically correct" to adjust the American way to the customs and language of other countries. It has become politically incorrect to give ballots in just English if there are a certain number of people in the voting area speaking a different language.

The matter of legislated multilingualism is not only divisive among people, but costly in government and business as their communications are by law required to be in multiple languages.

In some places such as South Florida resulting from the large influx of Spanish speaking people, this problem has risen to serious levels creating societal and economic problems.

Schools graduate students who can't speak nor write correctly in any one language. People remain divided culturally and in language creating tensions instead of cooperation.

It is my view that "political correctness" has escalated to such high levels that it deteriorates the economy, reduces cooperation between people and instills distrust in business and government. This has in a significant way contributed to the deterioration of America's society and world standing.

What matters far more than "what" we call each other is that we respect each other regardless of our differences. The strength of "us" collectively is how we use our differences to the benefit of "us". If on the other hand, we are afraid to recognize our differences, that weakens us as a society.

This means we need to focus more on being tolerant and respectful of others, no matter how different we may be, even if we don't look like the other or believe in the same philosophy. To reduce all of us to the same level is like in mathematics, constantly trending society lower and lower as it tries to find a common bottom. This unfortunately is the state I find America in as this book is written late 2014.

America's Collapsing Economy

The second millennium ushered into America financial disaster. Although the trigger to this disaster was the 9/11 terrorist attack , it was Washington's long term reaction that made it actually happen.

The country was in the process of ending a decade of economic growth and prosperity. The 9/11 terrorist attack shut down the stock market for an unprecedented week, the nations airlines were grounded and the nation went into shock. Although the country initially survived 9/11, it set into motion forces and government policies which eventually led to the:

- Technical bankruptcy of the U. S. government
- National credit crisis in 2008 forcing the failure of major Wall Street banks
- Bailout of GM along with the entire banking system
- Massive job losses with over 10% unemployment
- America's middle class labeled Americas new poor
- Median household income dropped 8% from 2007 to 2013. The top 1% in income received 93% of income gains significantly squeezing the middle class creating a new "almost poor class"
- Political upheaval and squabbles leading to eventual paralysis by congress which was unable to reach a federal budget eventually shutting down the government in 2013 when it was declared in technical bankruptcy.
- Loss of confidence in government to recover country
- Increasing economically driven violence

Leading the country into this abyss which became called "the Great Recession of 207-2008" included the U.S. invasion of Iraq in 2003 costing the country over a trillion dollars which led to the escalation of war into Afghanistan.

A second factor leading to this national financial crisis was the reduction in taxes by the first Bush administration which diminished tax revenues at the very time federal expenditures rose to historic heights resulting from the Iraq War.

This along with the longest recession since the Great Depression led to reduced tax income by the federal government eventually leading it to insolvency in 2013 as the congress would not raise the debt ceiling (borrowing limits) to cover current expenses.

The per capita income had since 9/11 been declining to becoming stagnant at best. But individuals offset declining income including job loss by refinancing their homes made possible by the real estate boom triggered by the super easy credit made available by banks through about 2006. When real estate values collapsed in 2007 sinking an average of 50% below their peaks and even as much as 75% in some markets, individuals mortgages became far in excess of the values of their homes.

At its worst, it was estimated that 43% of all homes in the United States were in this default stage which became known as "homes under water". Since incomes remained at best stagnant with massive layoffs seen, many homeowners could not make the high mortgage payments and were foreclosed by the banks, losing their homes. Some people even decided that their financial future would be better served if they preserved their cash and intentionally stopped making mortgage payments.

This had been unheard of as the home was the pillar of family financial security and the primary source for retirement income. When this new perception emerged, the banks adopted a defensive policy of offering "short sales" which allowed homeowners under certain conditions of hardship to sell their homes for less than was owed with the balance written off. But don't you cry for the banks. They were reimbursed by new federal stimulus programs and the already in place mortgage insurance paid for by the homeowners.

The combination of the massive loss of value in homes and the new ability to sell homes via the 'Short Sale" placed a massive new inventory of homes for sale which inhibited the recovery of housing values maybe for over a decade or more. By 2014, the housing values had recovered somewhat but nowhere close to what they were a decade earlier.

The belief that "My home is my best investment" had basically vanished and there was a flight to rentals. This transition to rentals was triggered by much tighter credit requirements for mortgages, a massive percentage of the population were given low credit scores due to personal credit problems, foreclosures and short sales and therefore no longer qualified for mortgages. The final nail in the housing ownership coffin was the continuing stagnation of family income along with the squeeze of the middle class.

By 2014, when I wrote this book, national unrest had risen to crisis levels. Family financial crises led to illness, suicides and a rising mental illness level. The drug industry experienced soaring sales of anti depressants while the mental health industry boomed.

All this was taking a toll on children who no longer felt the family security they once had and seeing what was happening to their parents, lost hope for their future. This rising insecurity and loss of hope for a better future led to increasing shootings in schools some even were massacres killing scores of students and teachers.

Racial unrest was increasing leading to street violence (Ferguson, Missouri). Increasingly was the rise of claims for discrimination by minorities who justified their violence by their poor economic status and loss of hope for better times.

Where did all this lead? By 2014, when I wrote this book, "Middle Class" or called by another name 'Main Street America" was in very poor shape. In far more families, both husband and wife had to work, more families had to downsize their living standards.

Even though the unemployment rate had dropped to 6% from 10%, there remained a rising number of workers who simply gave up looking or accepted new kinds of jobs at which they were lucky to get half of what they had in the former and forever lost career jobs.

The hope in 2014 was for the emergence of better leaders, the transition of a political system that became corrupt into one that once again would work. Will such leaders and recovery in political confidence emerge before the country collapses into chaos? That's the question I will answer in the final section of this book.

Obamacare - wrong turn in healthcare

No one doubted that the U.S. needed to do something about its health care system. This problem was not a new one. It just kept getting worse while congress continued its divisive debate resolving nothing.

More people were uninsured, estimated about 45 million and health care had become far more costly. But, just because 45 million were uninsured, that didn't mean they didn't have access to some form of health care. Many just went to the emergency room at the nearest hospital which was extremely expensive with the cost borne by public tax dollars and hospitals "eating" the cost by passing it to paying patients and increased billings to insurance companies. This process just increases health care costs even more making it unaffordable by more and more people thus adding to the uninsured problem and public tax burden.

So, the federal budget continued hovering at crisis levels resulting from:

- Dramatically rising costs of the Iraq & Afghan wars
- Reduced tax revenues thanks to the worst recession the country had seen since the Great Depression in the 30's
- Huge cost of bank bailouts and economic stimulus bailing out GM and others.
- Continuing congressional stalemate between Republicans and Democrats.

What did President Obama propose amidst this fiscal crisis? ? A gigantic and costly national health program supposedly making health care accessible and affordable by everyone. He was able to get congress to approve it only because House and Senate had a Democratic majority, despite not a single Republican voting in favor of this program, known as "Obamacare". This would eventually become the most divisive program ever and likely the main cause of the Government shutdown in 2013.

Obamacare, as structured, was so complex and convoluted that few, if anyone, including health care experts understood how it worked. When it finally was launched in 2013, the enrollment system consisting of websites didn't work, far more than anticipated were unable to enroll and many of those who were able to enroll found it more expensive than their prior insurance programs. Worse still, people who were insured prior to Obamacare were cancelled and offered a new policy often costing more and losing their present doctors. It was an absolute disaster and did not portray the U.S. well toward the rest of the world.

Should the government have taken steps to address the U.S. healthcare problem? Without a doubt, yes. But it should have done so in a two step program.

First, mandate that the health care industry adopt and accelerate the implementation of the new technologies already available. This could have been done with reimbursement and tax credit incentives. I personally proposed in 2007 a system I called "The virtual clinic" which dramatically would have improved medical diagnosis while significantly reducing costs. This would mandate the adoption of paperless medical records in a standard uniform format and the creation of central and universally accessible systems which estimate diagnoses using patient profiles and treatment outcomes.

The second phase should have been a simple universal and uniform health insurance program required by everyone in cooperation with employers and insurance companies. It does no one any good to have sick people coming to work spreading disease and doing poor work nor people forced to go to emergency hospital facilities for routine health issues.. Far better to offer clinics structured to provide comprehensive primary care. The net cost of such a system would have been far less to the tax payer than Obamacare and for sure, done a lot more to improve general health care.

But, the U.S. government insisted on pressing on with the super inefficient and costly system known as Obamacare portraying the U.S. as a country incapable of providing efficient health care for most Americans.

This alone sent a very negative signal to the world that United States is a country incapable of managing its own affairs. The leaders around seeing this were not impressed and thus, became less positive about America as a world leader.

Gunther Karger

Rising domestic violence

America has long been a leader in human rights as it expounds "human values" to the rest of the world. This has for long been a strong point in U.S. world leadership.

However ,this leadership became undermined as the world witnessed rising domestic violence triggered by loose gun controls, mass killings in schools by children and the Ferguson, Missouri allegation of police brutality. America was not portrayed well when a white police officer kills a black teenager for a minor infraction with all this followed by weeks of race riots and the display of military weapons to control civilian demonstrators.

China's Global Times said of this "*It's ironic that the U.S. with its brutal manner of assimilating minorities never ceases to accuse China and other countries of violating rights of minorities.*" The Russian Foreign Minister said "*U.S. needs to clean its own house if it wants to call itself the bastion of human rights*". Iran's Supreme Leader, the Ayatollah, criticized the U.S. for human rights abuses and Egypt's foreign minister urged the U.S. to use restraint and respect the right of people to peacefully assembly.

The Ferguson(St. Luis) incident followed the Trayvon Martin affair when a white vigilante stalked a black youth and killed him which enraged the black community.

The Ferguson incident illustrates a fundamental problem remaining in the U.S. where the highest unemployment rate is among the blacks as is the highest prison population. These remain serious domestic socio-economic problems which the world believes the U.S. should address more aggressively before reaching out to change the world.

Unfortunately, the rising trend of this domestic unrest has not helped America to sustain its historic leadership in human rights.

This, added to the collapse of the Congress to manage the affairs of the country seriously and negatively impacted America's position as a world leader.

The rising domestic unrest is a symptom of domestic economic problems where a middle class is squeezed and more people go without adequate food, jobs and health care. This situation was escalating during the first 15 years of the 21st Century contributing to civil unrest .

As of 2014 when this book was written, U.S. increasingly lost respect as a world leader and thus, continued to lose effectiveness as an agent for change. Example of this leadership change occurred on August 25 when a coalition of Egypt and United Arab Emirates Air Forces launched an attack against Islamist extremists in Libya without even informing the U.S. and worse still, surprising the U.S. While it is a very positive event indicating that the Arab nations finally have initiated taking charge of their own region's security, it illustrates the extent to which U.S. world leadership has deteriorated.

Another indication of declining U.S. influence in world affairs is the failure of its attempt to broker a cease fire in the 2014 Israel-Hamas war and the assumption by Egypt to undertake this task. It is additionally significant in this Egypt initiative in that Egypt was governed at that time by former Army Chief General Sisi. He had just been installed as president who threw out U.S. backed president Morsi whose brief one year rule nearly threw Egypt back into chaos.

All this once again confirms that a country must remain strong economically and politically to exert world leadership and that the U.S. was slipping in both respects.

Gunther Karger

Decline in technology leadership

When I went to engineering school in 1955, I don't recall seeing any foreign professors and there were a few students from other countries. Today, there are often more foreign born professors than Americans. During my professional time as an engineer in aerospace and communications, there were very few fellow workers and extremely few foreign born managers speaking broken English. This became reversed by 2014.

During my time working in the scientific field, the U.S. was without question a leader relative to companies doing the work and people working in the technology industries. This was particularly evident during the moon program in the sixties. Then, there were tech leading companies such as Bell Telephone Laboratories which pioneered all kinds of communications including satellites where I briefly worked. Bell Labs, a major company employing 20,000 people plus no longer exists except as a small remnant owned by Alcatel Lucent of France.

Before the present millennium, foreign students came to the U.S. to learn from American professors. This changed so dramatically by 2010 that many American students go to universities India because they are better. When I visited LSU in 2005 and was invited for lunch by the Dean of Electrical Engineering, he was Chinese. Today, much of the faculty there and many other universities are from China and other places in Asia many speaking broken English.

When I was invited to speak at the Globecom 2010 Conference, it was attended by nearly 3,000 engineers and scientists. The majority of all attendees and speakers were from countries other than the U.S. with a concentration from Asia. We had lunch with a professor of engineering at an Australian university who originally was from Amman, Jordan and whose name was Mohammad. The conference program chairman was Chinese and vice president of research for CISCO, one of the largest American companies in telecom equipment.

I had been invited to speak at this conference by an engineering professor at an Israeli university and the session chairman was from France.

Shirley & I had been invited to the occasional "Rocket Pioneers Gathering" at the Cocoa Beach Hilton in 2010. Gloom was evident among the 100 or so mostly retired astronauts and pioneers in space exploration and I am a member of this historic group. Why? President Obama had just announced the closing down of America's manned space program and had made a deal with Russia where Russian rockets would carry American astronauts to the International Space Station when the Space Shuttle operations would end in 2011. The conference was more like a wake for the space program we all once knew.

Shirley & I drove around Cape Canaveral area to see what was happening to the place where we once lived during the bustling Moon program. Houses were boarded up with overgrown lawns, stores were shut and streets were littered with For Sale and For Rent signs. This was the birthplace of America's exploration into space and where much of even today's technology was tested in space flights. It looked like the graveyard of the space program.

But let's not blame Obama for all this. The Space program and its related technology industry had been in decline for some years. Bush's Iraq war put budget pressures and the social scientists continued making greater inroads into government insisting that money is best spent on earth than outside it.

The big blame still goes to Obama because he missed out on a grand opportunity that not only would have saved the manned space program but created the basis for a more cooperative world. Just think what could have happened if instead of cancelling the American manned space program he would have engaged a few key foreign nations in a cooperative program. Not only would the U.S. have likely saved more by having other nations join in the project, technology development, that would have been stimulated economic benefits for all countries.

Such cooperative project would have resulted in Russia and the U.S. increase cooperation via the space program and potentially avoiding the near Cold War that evolved in 2014.

Even more important, the global economies badly in need of stimulus could have potentially been enhanced if they had been brought into the global space project. That would have led to more jobs, less poverty and less hunger all of which could have gone a long way to prevent many people from becoming terrorists. Hungry people without hope become criminals and this became an acute problem via the Arab Spring putting that entire region ablaze.

Obama and his people were so focused on the goal of making it better for the less fortunate that they lost sight of this grand opportunity. This could have become a latter day Moon Program and lest we forget, it was the ten year process of getting to the moon that brought the great technology advances and economic benefits. This became far more important than the actual Moon landing. The difference between "Then and now" (2014) is that then, the primary benefit was technology. Today, the primary benefit would have been greater global cooperation and a reduction in tensions between countries.

The wrong policy in space became another example of management by reaction rather than pragmatic planning and anticipating the future.

Impact of U.S. immigration policy

The politicians keep complaining about the 11 million undocumented people in the U.S. and the steady stream of people crossing our borders illegally. Well known is the practice of pregnant women finding their way across the borders showing up at U.S. hospital emergency rooms about to have their baby who, since it will be born in the U.S. will have special citizenship rights. In 2014, there was a rise in children being sent who illegally crossed the U.S. - Mexican border. These children didn't just come from Mexico but from all over Central America by parents who knew their kids could have a better life and be taken care of in the U.S.

Although this steady influx of immigrants provide a supply of workers which is good for American business, this increasing population places a burden on communities, particularly communities near the borders and the tax payers. The cost of feeding, housing and medical care for this increasing group of people becomes part of the tax burden on people increasingly being squeezed by lower to stagnant family incomes and property owners who already are stressed out by high property taxes.

What has Congress and the President done about this? More speeches and ideological debate. While the political debate goes on and on, the politicians continue to defer dealing with this problem until someone else is elected, Lets look at the numbers.

Based on U.S. Census data, the U.S. population in 2014 is estimated at about 315 million and I don't know if this includes the estimated 11 million undocumented immigrants. It definitely doesn't include the estimated 100,000 children who as of summer 2014 had managed to cross the border and are cared for by various U.S agencies awaiting immigration court decisions. Although it is difficult to estimate the total number of these undocumented people, it would be a logical conclusion that a high percentage of them receive social benefits from the U.S. be it federal assistance or local aid.

Gunther Karger

It Is estimated that the U.S. population will grow from the present 315 million to 400 million by 2050. This is a whopping 29% increase and about double the rest of the world. In fact, U.S. is listed in the same group of rapidly growing populations as Nigeria, Pakistan, Uganda, Ethiopia and India.

Based on the present demographics and assuming there will be no significant changes in immigration policy, it can be estimated that the majority of the 85 million population increase will come from that group of people. This will place on the economy an increasing economic and social burden on the American taxpayers and most likely increase demographically based tensions .

So what's the answer to this politically apparent unresolvable problem? Fortunately, the resolution will come from already in place global trends as are addressed in following chapters of this book. However, the U.S. can and should give more focus on assisting Central American countries in their economic development which ultimately will reduce the pressure of people leaving their own country. Another factor contributing to the resolution is the increasing awareness by foreign countries that the U.S. is trending to become less and less desirable.

On a near term basis however, it is essential that politicians address the current basic immigration problems. This includes at the minimum the enforcement of present rules and recognizing the existence of the 11 million undocumented people already in this country.

As a disclosure, I am a documented immigrant and a naturalized citizen.

Proactive vs Reactive Policy

The Ebola epidemic became a serious problem in the fall of 2014. Yes, the Ebola crisis is serious **but not** as serious as the continuing failure to be proactive about known problems and having to prepare recovery plans as the crisis evolves. Crisis planning starting when a crisis happens and developing fixes as it evolves is the worst possible situation to be in. Decisions generally are not the best, options are very limited and it generally is far more costly than having prepared for the crisis in advance. This report is about the need to be proactive about potential likely crisis situations and the need to prepare advance plans instead of waiting for the crisis to happen.

The current serious Ebola epidemic has been evolving and escalating for months. It should not have been a surprise because serious infectious diseases have been around since the beginning of time. In recent years, billions of Federal Dollars are spent annually on health. The Center of communicable Diseases (CDC) is assigned the responsibility for protecting the country against epidemics and various other federal and state agencies involved with public health. Yet, the country has not even had a Surgeon General for over a year as of the time the 2014 Ebola crisis evolved. The Surgeon General is supposed to lead the country's health policies as the country's Chief Medical Officer and for sure have in place an effective serious viral infection epidemic disaster plan. Neither a surgeon General nor such plan existed in the fall of 2014 when the Ebola epidemic hit.

This in principle is no different than reacting to the Hurricane Katrina disaster when the New Orleans levees broke instead of proactively fixing levees known to be deficient and likely to break during severe storms. There was no "if" about storms coming.

It was only "When" so there should have been a specific disaster plan in place to deal with a New Orleans flood and the levees should have been long before been brought to Hurricane Force 5 standards. After all, there existed "FEMA", the Federal Emergency Management Agency whose job it was to have such a plan. But there was none or at least none that worked.

Recalling space disasters, NASA knew that the "O" rings of the Challenger booster rockets were subject to failing during cold weather liftoffs but failed to Proact by proper redesign and then reacted when the Challenger blew up, killing the entire crew, costing the country billions with a serious setback in the space program.

The same happened with the Space Shuttle when NASA failed to proactively resolve the heat shield tiles falling off during liftoff causing Columbia to burn on re-entry with all lives lost.

During the months before 9/11, intelligence became clear that terrorist threats against the U.S were escalating and it was known that terrorists were training at flight schools learning to fly passenger jet aircraft. There even was specific intelligence pointing to imminent attacks against U.S. east coast major targets including the World Trade Center. Despite specific warnings from the CIA Ddirector of Counter Intelligence requesting elevation in threat level, the President's National Security Adviser(Condoleeza Rice) refused on the basis that aircraft attacks against public buildings had never before happened.

Had the security threat level been raised and an alert been issued for airport ticket agents to deny boarding of anyone on the terrorist list, chances would have been good that the terrorists would not have boarded the three aircraft at Boston possibly preventing the 9/11 disaster.

During the Cold War, it was known that both the Soviet Union and the United States had thousands of ICBM pointing at each other with the potential of one country initiating an attack.

Even though after years since this started no missile had been launched and it was improbable that this would happen due to the policy of "Detante", the Secretary of Defense ordered the creation of a small group of highly skilled scientists and intelligence specialists to deal with the improbable situation of handling an attack. This group of only about one hundred were assigned the job of developing systems and procedures reacting to a massive nuclear attack including launching a retaliatory attack against the Soviet Union. This group completed its mission and the country was ready for the attack that fortunately never happened. I was a key member of this group.

This was an example of "Proacting" vs "Reacting". We were ready if it happened and would have activated within minutes of an enemy nuclear missile launch the SIOP (Single Integrated Operational Plan) that prescribed what each assigned "post nuclear attack " recovery/retaliatory force participant was assigned to do. The country was ready, the planning had been done "proactively" before the potentially possible event. The disastrous planning during crisis was avoided.

The Centers for Communicable Diseases (CDC) should already have had a plan for dealing with Ebola and activated Phase One of the disaster plan as soon as the threat of such disaster even surfaced.   But no disaster plan had been prepared. The first step should have been to deny anyone with a U.S. passport from leaving a country with an Ebola outbreak to board an airplane or vessel with a U.S. itinerary. Phase one would also include the issue well planned Ebola Protocols to every U.S. hospital and emergency care facility. This would have been issued as soon as it became known that there was an Ebola outbreak in a specific country.

Following the Dallas hospital Ebola infections and learning that a health care worker directly treating a dying Ebola patient travelled freely on passenger planes exposing hundreds of passengers and people at airports, Congress held hearings to examine what happened.

Gunther Karger

The congressmen asked the CDC Director to develop plans preventing these things from happening in the future. Not having such plans already in action represents another example of the gross incompetence and neglectful management that appears to exist at federal government levels. If Congress has to deal with crises as they happen and evolve, the country itself is in an "incompetence crisis" which reflects a high level of inexperienced leadership within the U.S. government. This therefore, became another step downward in the international stature of America as a strong leader.

Global Trends

Since the beginning of time, progress has been driven by curiosity. The caveman adventured beyond the cave to see what was beyond the next mountain. The explorer searched for new lands, the scientist looked for better answers to the mysteries of the universe and the doctor looked for better ways to extend the quality of life.

Self preservation, curiosity and the drive for something better are inherent, instinctual characteristics of the human form. We are born with these instincts. We can use these creator given assets for good or evil. If we use it for good, we add improvement to the world. But if we use it for evil, we take from the world to benefit us individually at the expense of others. We see evidence of all this by examining history.

Fortunately, over time, good prevails over evil and we see a positive trend. To be sure, the road of history has not been a straight upward line. It has been a jagged road of time but long term, it is inexorable upward. This trend is driven instinctively by our inherent curiosity searching for more and better. The basic drivers are:

- Communications
- Transportation
- Science and Technology
- Curiosity about the unknown
- Self preservation

The prior section of my book dealt with the destructive forces seen in the early part of the 21 Century. This part of my book addresses the long term factors that have been in place and will continue into eternity. These are part of the fabric of the universe.

These basic drivers are transformative changing the world as we know from one generation to the next. Moreover, they are permanent as civilization expanded beyond the cave, beyond the mountain and oceans and we already have begun searching beyond our planet called Earth.

Although in 2014 we seem to be in a declining world moving toward some kind of abyss, rest assured that the abyss will suddenly appear as a golden hill. Those of future generations will have more as our individual worlds reach out globally and beyond into space. Rest assured, the universe as fantasied by the likes of Jules Verne, Isaac Asimov, Arthur C. Clarke and Robert Heinlein called science fiction during their lifetimes is already becoming transformed into reality.

No matter how bad things seem to be today in 2014 when we see the Mideast collapsing driven by the destructive forces of ISIS and country leaders being obsessed with containing terrorism, better times lay ahead. This is the inherent trend not only here on Earth, but in the universe. Learn and trust history and its lessons.

Now, read on to see how I use the science of PHM (Psychohistorical Morphology) to project how this will evolve beyond the current crisis.

Technology accelerates Globalization

Mobility is what enabled the primitive man to move beyond his cave using horses overland and boats on water. This gradually improved into trans ocean rowed longboats improved by the Viking, Erik the Red in the 9th century enabling him to leave Norway reaching Iceland and Greenland. Further refinements of his longboat design enabled him and his Vikings to become the first to reach North America in Newfoundland about 500 years before Columbus officially discovered America using his new transocean crossing large sailing ships driven by wind. The world became discovered further using the Sextant discovered by Isaac Newton making it possible to navigate by the stars. These ships carried not only people but cargo stimulating world trade. Overland travel expanded with horse driven wagons later by trains, cars and trucks.

During the past 100 years we learned how to transport people and cargo by huge ships and aircraft capable of transporting 600 people in one airplane and whole trucks in cargo planes in just a few hours to anyplace on earth. Over the past 50 years, we learned to reach out into space with rockets and landed astronauts on the moon. Today, a private space transportation company is taking reservations and selling tickets for the first commercial space flights and over the next 25 years, we will see routine space flights.

As people were able to travel further at increasing speeds, the ability to communicate became the limiting factor. Early communications were carried out by couriers delivering messages by mouth later by hand carried dispatches. The range and speed was increased by using pigeons carrying notes.

A giant leap in communications occurred on December 12, 1901 when Marconi, the Italian engineer demonstrated long range radio communications across oceans.

The transmitter in the UK used a 500 ft. antenna hoisted into the air by a kite and the receiver in Newfoundland, 2200 miles distant detected three clicks represented the letter "S" in Morse Code.

This became the first transoceanic radio communication. Marconi went on to found Cable and Wireless which pioneered radio communications with the company still existing today.

Today, our world depends on communications via land lines, radio and satellites. We are well along the way of physically disconnecting ourselves by having handheld radio driven devices allowing us to talk with each other no matter where on earth we may be, do business using computers and visually see not only each other but images of the products we are buying and selling.

Communications and computer usage is exploding worldwide making every place on earth in communication range within seconds. Communications is bringing industry and commerce even to remote villages perched high in the Andes of South America, deep the Amazon river jungle, the steppes of Central Asia and remote islands in the Indian Ocean.

The combination of the exploding means of communications particularly in the wireless mode enabling a high degree of mobility and the increasing fast and efficient means of travel is bringing the world closer together. Today, we see that's happening regardless of where we are at the moment and where it's happening right on our TV screen nearly while it's happening. And, the TV screen can be a large 50 inch TV in your home or a small 3 inch screen in your hand and soon on your wrist.

This is what's enabling and accelerating globalization among people and nations. Although politicians still try to isolate and insulate their countries from the rest of the world and its relentless coming together, the expanding role of technology prevents this from succeeding.

My Life – Global Society Rising

As technology accelerates and expands, the natives in the most jungle villages or on isolated islands in the midst of the Pacific Ocean will see the quality of life will improve exponentially.

The things which the developed 20% of the world's population consider necessities today are gradually just being discovered as luxuries to the rest of 80% of the world's 7 billion population. This places an immense and long term demand for products and services to satisfy the emerging needs and increasingly, the ability to finally discover a better life for nearly 6 billion people.

The good news is that no matter what the politicians attempt to reverse this trend trying to maintain control over people and countries, they will fail. What will prevail is the increasing and irreversible trend of more and more people of diverse location and background to coexist and prosper. Those who resist this trend will fail as leaders, as businesses, countries and individual persons.

Those who fail to recognize this irreversible trend violate the most basic law of the universe. Time is irreversible and the hands of the clock always move forward to the right. Leaders who don't heed this natural law will fail. Their companies eventually go out of business as their products become outdated, national leaders will be replaced as the people unseat them either by election or force and yes, individuals destroy themselves vis mental illness trying desperately to regain the past. The past is gone, forever or at least, until the time machine is invented.

We as individuals, members of a community or citizens of a country should never forget that the trend toward globalization will always continue, that technology will always change how we work and live. Finally beyond our lives, this trend will continue as mankind reaches beyond the world we today know as "Earth".

Gunther Karger

Evolution of Global Terrorism

Until recently and historically, there were three forms of violence and the purpose of these three were very different:

- Wars were waged between tribes and countries generally to resolve territorial disputes, enforce religious views and achieve change within given boundaries. Wars within the same countries or tribes generally within the same geographical area were and continue to be known as civil wars which is a gross misnomer because civil wars within a country can be more brutal than wars between countries.
- Criminal actions involving murders, theft, extortion, kidnapping, rape, economic crimes
- Terrorism evolving in recent years consists of a few people, sometimes just one person, terrorizing innocent people unrelated to a cause to create notice for a cause. Terrorism in the name of a cause has no boundaries and can be committed by children as well as adults

While wars are generally territorial and broadly based with opposing sides identifiable by different uniforms, language or even racial characteristics, crimes are very localized down to individuals with the perpetrators not distinguishable by uniform. These forms of violence have existed since the beginning of time and most likely will continue even in the unlikely situation wherein there is total peace in all the earth because then wars and conflict likely will be with alien forces.

Wars are characterized by each side prevailing over the other settling their differences depending on who can inflict enough damage on the opposing side. Wars get settled or just end when either the losing side gives in because of unacceptable loss of life and damage or the winning side runs out of resources to continue.

The Thirty Year War(1618-1648) was ended by the brutal Russian winter which killed most of the invading soldiers from Western Europe. Eventually, when wars have spent itself themselves out, both sides settle the dispute by agreeing to concessions, mostly by the losing side. Crimes on the other hand are settled by police catching and punishing the criminals with applicable laws.

Each of these three forms of violence involve varied forms of terrorism because people are terrorized by the onslaught of a column of gun smoking tanks destroying anything in their way of bombs falling from the sky with similar impact. But there is nearly nothing more terrorizing than a teenager walking by with a backpack that suddenly explodes killing and injuring hundreds and setting buildings on fire.

Over the past 50 years, terrorism has evolved. Groups seeking some change and unable to achieve it by peaceful means uses violence as a means of scaring the general public thus putting pressure on government leaders to give these people what they want. This is nothing more than extortion by violence except the violence is perpetrated against innocent bystanders and the creation of civil havoc.

The deliverers of this type of violence typically are people like ourselves, even teenagers and can be male or female. They typically place bombs in public places such as restaurants, airports, hotels and detonate these remotely or by timers or more recently, by becoming themselves suicide bombers in the belief they will become martyrs and go to their heaven. The hijacking of passenger airplanes has been a favorite tool of terrorists because their demands then must be met immediately holding the passengers as hostages.

Terrorists as defined as the "terrorists" as we perceive originated after the establishment of the State of Israel. Anti Israel groups began their terrorism by hijacking passenger airplanes terrorizing the passengers while making their demands to political powers for the Jews to leave the areas they took in the wars.

Forgotten was the fact that the lands were in each instance occupied in the defense from attacking Arab Forces. Terrorists often kidnap significant politically involved people demand ransom to fund their operations.

Terrorists can take the form of the famous "Carlos the Jackal" who operated as a lone wolf on behalf of causes. Recent causes include crime syndicates such as the Russian Mafia, the well known Al Quaeda led by deceased Osama bin Laden and the newly formed Buku Haram in Africa.

President George W. Bush concluded that Saddam Hussein, the Iraq dictator was somehow responsible for the 9/11 attack and was preparing for more terrorist attacks against the U.S. Nothing could have been further from the facts or truth.

The reality was that Hussein, as bad as he might have been, kept strict law and order in Iraq and the arch enemies of Sunni and Shia Islamic factions from killing each other while keeping Iran busy with the eight year Iraq - Iran war.

Invading Iraq in a classical territorial war to unseat its government should go down in history as the worst strategic blunder of the century. Not only did the U.S. get rid of the primary stabilizing force in that part of the world, but it triggered a sequence of events which unleashed terrorist forces never before seen. The chaos caused by the toppling of Saddam Hussein was followed by the failure of the U.S. to install a strong temporary regime. This blunder led to the self destruction by civil war which created at least a million new jihadists hating the U.S. like no one ever had before. This formed the basis of the ISIS terrorists what emerged in 2014 and overtook large parts of Iraq and Syria.

The "Arab Spring" started in Tunisia triggered by the street vendor putting himself into flames spreading into Syria where a few terrorists tried to overthrow the Assad regime which had maintained order for many years. In Syria, the U.S. made its second worst blunder. By not supporting the Assad regime which kept order and trying to broker a deal for more freedom by the people, it unleashed one of the worst bloodsheds in the Mideast.

The worst result of the U.S, blunder was that its "standoff no strategy policy" paved the way for the Iraqi terrorists to combine with extremist religious fanatics in Syria to form ISIS, Islamic state of Iraq and Syria. This terrorist group came into Iraq, overran the Iraqi army, stole its modern weapon arsenal supplied by the U.S. and declared itself as the ISIS Caliphate. As of the fall of 2014, ISIS became the most radical and most dangerous terrorist group ever having managed itself to become a state, with its own army and fanatical leader.

As of this writing, fall 2014, ISIS continues expanding carving out its caliphate state out of Syria and Iraq enforcing its brutal regime over the people. This is an example of what happens when terrorism is allowed to grow and metastasize into a national state posing a threat to neighboring countries and yes, the rest of the world.

This also happens when the U.S. doesn't exercise leadership in effectively dealing with terrorism which it has not. Clearly, this can't be allowed to continue.

So what must be done to finally resolve this problem and reduce terrorism to the localized level it always has seen and always will? The world leading powers, such as they may be and as evolve over time, must realize that terrorism of the form such as it has become is unacceptable. They should form a unified world anti terrorist group empowered to deal with terrorists whoever they may be and wherever they may be operating.

In the case of ISIS and the Mideast, the U.S. should take leadership in forming a coalition of itself, European and Mideast countries including Israel to eradicate ISIS and the likes. The U.S. should also revaluate its policy of trying to enforce its form of freedom onto other countries for which it does not work culturally nor practically.

The new policy should be to support stability and for Syria, that's the Assad regime. Like it or not, it is the regime which for many years maintained a stable country. The new policy should be to support stability as top priority because without stability there comes chaos.

The U.S. should finally learn the lessons of history and from the huge mistakes made since the 9/11 terrorist attack.

The U.S. should also adopt a policy recognizing that freedom means different things to different cultures and start to respect that. Freedom to do whatever one wants to do simply no longer works in a multicultural global society that's being forced to work and exist together.

It doesn't even work right here in the U.S. If a strong leader doesn't soon emerge in the U.S. it might itself experience rising civil unrest to the level that eventually leads to a change in how it governs itself ending the country once known as "America, land of the free".

War and Crime

Since the beginning of time, wars settled territorial disputes and was the tool of aggression. It didn't matter whether the conflict was between tribal disputes, the expansion of borders or annexing distant lands by creating colonies. The aggressor whether it be ruled by tribal chief, a king, dictator or republic traditionally had as a primary goal to occupy and rule property and the wealth that it contained be it gold, oil or strategic geographic location.

Over time, wars were waged between countries to change borders or exert political control such as occurred during the era of the Soviet Union when politically controlled countries were called "satellites". The Soviet Union was nothing more than an expanded Russia empire controlling many republics in Central Asia and Eastern Europe. An example of this was Hungary when its government tried to become independent of Soviet political control; and the Russian army with its tanks rolling into Budapest to secure its control.

The tools of classical warfare were originally soldiers marching led by cavalry on horses which led cannons on wheels on land and fleets extending these beyond their shores on ships. The foot wars eventually led to battles between cannon equipped ships on the sea and aerial battles between fighter airplanes trying to keep heavy bombers from destroying cities and factories. Territorially driven wars continue to this day seeing Russia just having annexed the Crimean Peninsula where Russia had based its Black Sea navy and continuing this into the adjacent Ukraine to secure a land bridge to Crimea Peninsula jutting out into the Black Sea. This gives the Russians access to the Mediterranean Sea.

Over recent years, warfare has expanded beyond territorial conquest to enforcing ideology and religion over others. Ideological conflicts have always existed since the beginning of time and some territorial wars such as the Thirty Year War were triggered by religious conquest.

However, the 9/11 attack launched against the United States by al Quaeda, the terrorist group based in Afghanistan triggered what became known as "The war against Terrorism". When President George W. Bush launched a counter attack with airplanes, missiles and giving support to tribal chiefs who already were trying to overthrow the Afghanistan Taliban government which harbored the terrorists, the 'War on Terrorism" leapt beyond borders and uniformed armed forces.

Osama bin Laden's attack was carried out with just a dozen young people. They hijacked American commercial airplanes boarded them in Boston to then flew two airplanes directly into the New York World Trade Center destroying it and killing over 3,000 people. Another hijacked airplane, at the same time, was flown into the Pentagon in Washington killing hundreds and inflicting major damage on the massive building. This triggered what we in 2014 know as the "War on Terrorism" which became defocused when the U.S. policy erroneously tried to bring it back to the traditional warfare principles by invading Iraq and later, re-invading Afghanistan.

By 2014, thirteen years after the 9/11 attack using hijacked American airplanes, the newly formed ISIS moved across the Syrian border into Iraq and the stole billions of Dollars of modern warfare equipment the U.S. had given Iraq to defend itself with. Now, armed with tanks, personnel carriers, missiles and tons of current technology arms, ISIS in just a few months became an army of more than 20,000 well organized terrorists. They ran over most of northern Iraq and declared the territorial Islamic State of Iraq and Syria to become the new Caliphate of all of Islam led by its leader who became the latter day "Caliph".

The U.S. reaction to this new terrorist group was to launch air strikes from carriers based just offshore and sending a few U.S. military advisors to help the Iraqi military cope with this new threat. ISIS retaliates by starting to behead American journalists held hostage and display this beheading in public view on U Tube for the world to see on TVs and computer screens.

These barbarians also invaded villages of Christians and tribes believing in various forms of religions killing them in horrible ways unless they convert to the ISIS created barbaric Sunni form of Islamic belief.

Meanwhile, in the jungles of West Central Africa, the Boko Haram terrorists kidnap hundreds of young school girls to become sex slaves unless the Nigerian government meets their demands. In 2014, the Pakistani government launched a new offensive against the Taliban which had basically taken over the Waziristan province from which they are directing the resurging civil war in Afghanistan trying to retake control over that country.

As of this book being written late 2014, the world is increasingly being fractured by a combination of ideologically based terrorists who operate like crime gangs equipped with high tech tools of warfare. Yes, I call them criminals because what else can they be called when they steal., extort and commit massacres and murder by beheading innocent hostages?

It seems also that world leaders have yet to come to grips with this growing problem even though without question it has reached crisis levels. The president of the United States even went on TV to declare that he has yet not formulated a strategy on how to deal with this and just days after this statement, ISIS issues yet another U tube video showing the beheading of a second American journalist held hostage. Meanwhile, Obama flies to Europe for discussions about what to do about the increasing efforts by Russia's President Vladimir Putin's escalating military invasion into the Ukraine after his Russian sponsored Ukrainian separatists shoot down a Malaysian commercial airplane filled with about 300 passengers and crew.

What does the world need to address this evolving crisis? It's really simple. The answer lies in the nearest police station. What does the police do when there is a rise in murders, theft and intentional destruction of property in the commission of crimes?

The police chief does what police chiefs do. He assigns officers to go out and deal with the problem and importantly, work with other agencies to identify the criminals, apprehend them and turn them over to the justice system. The police chief has to be a leader taking charge. He would become the laughing stock of the community if he went before the camera and said 'I don't yet have a strategy for dealing with this crime". Sure, he might not have a strategy in an evolving crime spree but he would never say that to the public.

So what's really needed to deal with this new wave of international terrorism? It's actually quite simple.

- Declare the terrorist acts as the crime they are, being murder, mass destruction of property, kidnapping hostages, extortion, massive theft and horrendous violation of basic civil rights.
- Organize a task force of local, national and international law enforcement, military and intelligence resources focused on resolving this terrorist problem and give this task force the resources to deal with it effectively.
- Take leadership and ownership of this problem but work closely with other countries to create an international effort that remains effective as deterrent against future acts of terrorism.
- Provision this task force with the latest technology and keep that current going forward to prevent terrorists from getting an upper hand.

Would this be easy? No but then, if it were easy, it would have been already done and I wouldn't need to include this chapter in this book. What is easy however is to exert leadership. The missing thing is a person capable of being such leader, as of the time this book is written, 2014.

Revolution in military systems

The foot soldier, horse drawn cannon, sail driven frigate were replaced by motorized personnel carrier, troop transport ships, airplanes and missiles. These military systems over thousands of years had one element in common. They were soldier intensive relying on armies occupying land and mobile vessels controlling sea and air space.

We are today entering another revolution where these are being replaced by the tools of science and technology. Until recently, it might have been required to send in an invasion force and a fleet of aircraft supported by a naval battle group to resolve conflicts between countries, we are entering an age of an entirely new kind of warfare.

Instead of an "army" of spies in foreign countries gathering intelligence known as "Humint' (human intelligence), we are increasingly using surveillance by electronic means and satellite observations. Very localized drones and UAV's (unmanned aerial vehicles) already are making the transition of just intelligence gathering to replacing the role of fighter jets and light bombers.

In past wars, the enemy was easily identifiable by uniform and location. Today, more and more, it's getting difficult to tell the difference between enemy and friend. The person walking next to you down the street could be wearing a suicide vest and blow up the entire block or building. Passengers today are screened by machines and physical inspections before allowed to board airplanes and increasingly before being allowed entry to public buildings such as courthouses, theatres and train stations. Today, we have to be less concerned about an enemy warship entering one of our ports than a lone wolf terrorist carrying a backpack with a small nuclear bomb or radioactive device capable of killing thousands.

Yes, we are indeed entering a new era in warfare. A lot of the massive manpower is being replaced by new technology and the destructive force per "soldier" is increasing massively. Instead of a fleet of troop ships delivering army and Marine divisions to a foreign country, we will more and more deploy special operations units via air drops or helicopter to deal with specific threats. Replacing an entire forward operations communication unit, one special ops person goes in with a satellite communications back pack which provides a ground cell network for the entire special operations group and links it to HQ via the satellite com unit. Such 'Rapid Deployment" special ops units already are becoming deployable to any place on earth within 48 hours.

The long range heavy billion dollar bomber is being replaced by hypersonic unmanned aircraft capable of delivering a 2000 lb plus ordnance payload destroying targets with pin point accuracy any place on the globe within hours of launch. As of 2014 when this book is written, prototypes of the X51A hypersonic UAV has already been tested proving the feasibility of this capability.

Ordnance capable drones are increasingly replacing pilot flown tactical missions to destroy small targets be they terrorist camps in Afghanistan or military convoys on the move. Satellite based highly destructive laser beams will over the next decade be capable of destroying major ground targets within minutes of deploy orders by the general to a ground based command center.

Many foreign located airbases will become obsoleted by large aircraft/missile based sea based ships/platforms which can be deployed to the nearest offshore location. These platforms can support operations in most potential combat areas and already are serving as off shore bases in the Gulf region supporting air strikes in the Iraq/Syria operations against ISIS.

Gone will be the time when marginal people having problems finding work resolve their employment or personal problems by just signing up for the military.

They must either already be highly trained for the new high tech tasks of the new warfare or tested trainable and sent to schools to learn new skills.

Future military operations will become far more multi national especially in the tasks of controlling terrorists. This can and eventually will lead to much greater multi national cooperation which over time will stimulate the economies of many nations.

I foresee educational systems starting to offer certificates and degrees in military science as the demand for far more highly trained personnel will be needed by the military. This likely will become a bonanza for the technical/vocational level schools as the focus will be on specific skills far more than academic studies.

A significant new manpower resource for future warfare exists in the rapidly increasing reduction of troops and personnel no longer needed in the Afghan/Iraq wars. Instead of offering these veterans social services such as unemployment, offer them training for their next but far different military assignments. The classical and present typical soldier's physical demands leads to their retirement at an early age. However, the new military missions are more based on non physical skills thus dramatically extending the useful lives of military personnel. These people already know a lot about the military and just need to be taught new and mostly technical skills.

Finally, I see a return to space for future military systems not only for earthbound defense but also for defense against space borne threats such as asteroids. I see a future of space based rapid deployment stations to support far more than destructive laser beam systems.

The challenge over the next several years will be to find the politicians and government leaders capable of understanding and managing this transition into the future. As of 2014, this has become a huge problem given the political disaster facing the U.S. Senior political leadership has reached an extraordinary level of incompetence.

Gunther Karger

Cyberworld and privacy

What would we do without computers? Worse still, what would we do without Internet access?. Heaven help us if we lost our cell phone. How would we rent a car, book an airline reservation or hotel without a credit card? Send an email, tweet or denied paying bills online?

The answer is simple. We couldn't. Our world is based on communications and credit cards. Unless you want to find a time machine and travel back to the stone age, our existence is based on these and will increasingly depend on these.

What about privacy? We have less and less and that's like it or not. That's a fact. Every time we use the credit card, that transaction is processed to buy what we just selected, debit one of our accounts, give our name, address etc to the shipper and it goes into a file that remembers this transaction for marketing and accounting purposes. When we make a telephone call, that's recorded by the telephone company and when we send an email, our email address is recorded by the Internet provider. When we see the doctor, our social security number is recorded along with all kinds of medical data. Every time we fill up the gas tank using a credit card, the gas station, credit, card processing company and the issuing bank will know where we were at that instant.

That's life. The way it is and there isn't much we can do about it unless we crawl into a cave never to use a phone, computer or car. Does this mean we share some of our private information? You bet it does but there isn't much we can do about it if we want to live a normal life. Do we have to be careful how we use this system, to whom and how we give this information? Yes, very careful. The best protection we can give ourselves is to know how the systems and services we use work.

Could someone steal any of this data about yourself? Of course, yes. Just like someone could pick your wallet, swindle you out of money in a scam or steal your car. But if your wallet or your car is stolen, you report it to the police and expect the police to use all its resources to catch the criminal and get your car or your money back, You don't give a second thought about the vast resources the police have these days investigating crime and indeed hope they have the best there is.

Let's right now go to cybercrime which are crimes relative to the world of cyberspace encompassing computers, communications and the internet. What we just addressed is personal cybercrime including identity theft and stealing money from your bank account via the Internet.

This has evolved and expanded into serious problems because the cyberthief who emptied your bank account or filed false medical claims on your behalf could be anywhere in the world such as China and Russia. Cybercrime knows no borders or language barriers because the medium of cybercrime is the Internet which is global.

Over the past few years, cybercrime has expanded into major industrial cyber invasion of corporate data systems stealing trade secrets and government computer systems. This then expanded to stealing military secrets and other government sensitive information. This should be called what it is and that is cyber-espionage.

A more recent form of cybercrime is invading the Electric Grid which generates, distributes and controls the electric and gas utility industry. Cybercriminals today have the capability to hack and exert control of electricity transmission and nuclear power plants.

In recent years, cybercrimes have attracted very serious attention of law enforcement, banks, utilities, transportation, military and intelligence agencies.

The National Security Agency (NSA) and CIA have massive counter cybercrime efforts while the military recently established its new "Cyber Command".

Then along came Edward Snowden who proclaimed himself the champion of privacy by individuals against any surveillance using cybertools. He declared it against privacy rights for the government to listen in on phone conversation and in fact any electronic eavesdropping. He did this while an employee at the NSA where he himself stole vast amounts of secret data and then leaked it to the media declaring that the government had no legal right to obtain such data.

What was Snowden? He was a traitor of the worst kind. Not only did he take it upon himself to steal secret data from his employer, the government and leaked that information to parties which could harm the U.S. , he disclosed to the world and America's enemies thus far secret cyber processes. Knowing now how the U.S. operates its own cyber surveillance systems, America's enemies can adjust their terrorist networks in ways very difficult to detect. The NSA was forced to develop and implement alternate information surveillance systems so that the enemies would find it difficult to hack and evade U.S. government systems. The cost alone for this has been estimated in the Billions not even considering the degraded national security systems this leaker caused.

Concurrently and accelerating triggered by the Snowden affair, the civil rights organizations and people supporting such organizations dramatically escalated their efforts into any targeting of U.S. citizens and pushed to their limit their objections electronic surveillance. This continued and escalated even as the world is facing increased threats by terrorist organizations such as ISIS with Russia returning to Cold War activities against Western Europe and the U.S.

All this raises the fundamental question: "Why should the U.S. and its security organizations be severely limited in its fight against cybercrimes, cyber threats against national security when the cyber criminals and foreign intelligence organizations and operatives use whatever means they can develop and they are very capable?"

Why should the U.S. hamper its own anti cybercrime efforts when cyber criminals round the world are reaching right into our own pockets, industrial systems and government agencies? Why should we limit the NSA and the new military cybercommand in its efforts to defend the country and protect its citizens?

Surely a reasonable balance between individual privacy and the right to crime fighting and national security can be found. What good is a high level of personal privacy when that has been taken to such extreme that national security has been compromised?

It is my view that over the next few years, cyber crime will become an increasingly serious threat to personal and national security and its industry will see a dramatic increase in funding and personnel. Cybercrime fighting will become an increasingly important economic stimulus and we all should be supportive and thankful for that instead of fighting it in the name of privacy.

Gunther Karger

Globalization of economies

The trend toward the global economic village continues to accelerate driven by advancing communications, more efficient shipping and monetary systems. Distributed manufacturing in particular is driving global commerce. This results from designing products in one country, manufacturing the parts in multiple countries even on different continents and then shipping the parts to assembly plants at locations strategic to the markets. This is illustrated by the JIT(Just in time) systems whereby parts are ordered and shipped to assembly plants all in widely different global locations just in time for their need to be installed.

An example of this principle is this book. If you ordered it online on a website, immediately after the order is processed and payment is approved by your bank or credit card, a computer generated message goes to a printer which has the electronic file comprising the manuscript of this book and prints it into the physical book you receive in a few days. This is "printing on demand", book by book instead of printing thousands of books with an expensive inventory in book stores and incurring time consuming and costly physical shipping.

The interlinking of commerce and economies will increasingly become the driver for greater international cooperation and trade alliances between countries. This factor is becoming significant in the need for countries with different political systems to cooperate more than fighting with each other. Except for terrorist controlled countries which by 2014 have evolved to a high level in more countries, cooperation will be increasingly becoming more common than wars. Economic sanctions will become increasingly more effective in resolving conflicts or at least minimizing military destructive processes.

The common economic interest by more and more nations will force them to cooperate more and more. More and more we will see alliances to engage in multinational military actions to deal with nations controlled by terrorist groups such as ISIS and isolationist countries such as North Korea.

As the global populations increases by about 2 billion from the present 7 billion to 9 billion by the year 2050, the globalization of individual economies will be even more pronounced. Global growth will become driven by accelerated attention to resolve environmental problems, food production and the construction and reconstruction of basic infrastructure such as roads, bridges, water supplies and flood controls.

In the next decade, more and more isolationist nations will realize that the cost of remaining isolated and maybe even controlled by fanatical governments can far exceed the benefits of economic worldwide cooperation.

"The best weapon against terrorism is food and jobs delivered via a globalized economy."

"Hunger and unemployment fans the fires of terrorism". Gunther Karger, 2014

Declining Freedom

There is no such thing as total freedom which so many people seek. What's more, we'll see less and less personal freedom as population grows and more and more people are forced to coexist in increasingly more congested places. Let's get some perspective on freedom since the beginning of time.

- The caveman 50,000 years ago was subject to no laws. But his life depended on his ability to hunt for his daily food while he himself was hunted by wild animals and subject to severely wild storms and earthquakes. Was this caveman "free" to do as he pleased or restricted by the laws of nature?
- A resident in a gated community complains because he isn't allowed a large attack dog in his condo. Is this unreasonable suppression of his freedom?
- A cigar smoker lights up in a restaurant and is asked to leave or put it away. Is this limiting his rights to whatever it is he wants or respecting the right of other guests to avoid breathing cancer producing smoke?
- The Iranians revolted against their Shah because they wanted "freedom" from his oppressive regime and replaced him with their Ayatollah and Islamist extremists. Did they become "free"? Absolutely not. They became more controlled. The same happened in Egypt where the demonstrators threw out the president and elected their own who turned out to be just another Islamist who a year later was thrown out by the military. Is this freedom?
- The Libyans revolted against their dictator Muammar Quadaffi and in his place got a country of chaos ruled by terrorist gangs. When Quadaffi was overthrown, the bells of freedom rang in Libya. Two years later the people can't leave their house in fear of being killed.

- If you drive on a farm road where there is no traffic, you have the freedom to test the speed limit of your car engine even if you can get it up to 150 mph. But are we allowed to do this downtown endangering other city street drivers?

Freedom is a relative thing that must be assessed in context of one's particular situation. A passenger on a large 5000 passenger mega cruise ship has much less freedom than the passenger on a barefoot sailing yacht where if he chooses to lay naked on the deck, he could unless a large fish pops up to sample the view or gets its lunch.

Remember Napoleon? He overthrew the French king to get freedom for his people in the French Revolution. A century of bloodshed followed.

Today in the U.S. a rising number of unemployed and under privileged people demand more freedom to do as they choose. But what about the rest of the people? They have to work harder to pay the taxes needed for sustaining the unemployed spending their time marching in the streets for freedom instead of working at some job feeding themselves?

People who seek freedom should first look at history and honestly assess their circumstances before demanding to get what they want. If they get their wish, they might just want to get back the freedom they once had.

Gunther Karger

Historical perspective 2001-2015

The 9/11 terrorist attack was a historic event that would have profound impact on our personal lives and set the world into a new direction. This terrorist attack against the U.S committed by just dozen terrorists hijacked four commercial airliners and flew two of them at full speed into the World Trade Center in New York totally destroying them along with killing 3300 people. The third aircraft few into the Pentagon seriously damaging "Fortress America" killing hundreds triggered the beginning of a changed world. The fourth airplane targeted the White House but was overtaken by passengers causing it to crash into a Pennsylvania field killing all aboard.

No, it wasn't the terrorist act itself that led to the massive forward change that eventually led to today. It was how the United States reacted to it that made the difference. The failure to react maturely to this very serious challenge to America's security was largely based on the lack of historical perspective by America's leaders then and now in power.

President George W. Bush instead of focusing on the terrorists perpetrating this horrendous act seeking them out and destroying them in a police style operation, launched the 'War on Terrorism" targeting entire countries starting with the invasion of Afghanistan which government harbored Osama bin Laden's Al Quaeda terrorist group. He correctly aided anti-government tribal leaders toppling the brutal Taliban regime and helped form a new moderate government.

But, instead of focusing on going after the terrorists who perpetrated the 9/11 attack, he diverted his attention to Iraq declaring its dictator a world enemy threatening the U.S. and the rest of Western World. He declared that Iraq was imminently about to use weapons of mass destruction against the U.S. which later were found not to exist.

This diversion into Iraq allowed Osama bin Laden's terrorist group to seek refuge in the rugged mountains on the Pakistan border. What should have taken a few months at most to locate and neutralize this terrorist group took 8 years and it was a commando operation of just a few U.S. Special Forces soldiers that accomplished this.

Two years after the limited U.S. incursion into Afghanistan and before finishing the job of destroying Osama bin Laden and his people, President Bush launched a war against Iraq for the purpose of toppling its dictator, Saddam Hussein. Instead of using the effective tools of empowering Hussein's internal enemies and helping them resolve their internal political problems, Bush launches a classical warfare starting with massive air strikes and tanks with ground forces following all the way into Baghdad.

The first mistake Bush made was to invade Iraq to topple Hussein. Had he studied history, he would have easily realized that this was one of the worst actions that could be taken. By toppling Hussein, he removed the primary force stabilizing that part of the world as Hussein and Iran were bitter enemies fighting an eight year war killing over a million people on both sides. But, this war kept Iran and its fanatical Shia government busy not developing a nuclear capability while limiting its support of the Hamas and Hezbollah terrorist groups which were continually trying to destroy Israel.

Removing Hussein and worse still, dismantling the then in place strong Iraq army and central government and handing anarchy over to a weak Shia leader (Malaki) empowered Iran to shift its resources from Iraq to trying destroying Israel via Hamas and Hezbollah took this mistake to the extreme. Looking back, this turned out to be a serious political blunder by U.S. foreign policy.

The second mistake was to allow Iraq to fall into chaos and a sectarian civil war and then leave it to be handled by Malaki, a known weak leader. This triggered the rise of terrorists within Iraq spawned by a new hatred of the U.S. which had invaded their possibly oppressed but peaceful country.

The U.S. invasion and subsequent 11 years of occupation led to a civil war largely destroying Iraq, killing a hundred thousand civilians and causing nearly three million people to flee. Among these were many young people hating the U.S seeking revenge and become jihadists and future terrorist, many of who became the ISIS jihadists of 2014.

The Iraq war cost Americans at least a trillion dollars, the death of over 3,000 soldiers and probable became a trigger to the U.S. budget crisis which materially contributed to the 2007-2010 financial crisis becoming the worst recession since the Great Depression. The irony was that as of 2014, a year after U.S. troops were withdrawn, President Obama started sending military people back to save Iraq from its new enemy, the Islamic State of Iraq and Syria (ISIS)

America's defective foreign policy was also not helped when Obama went to Egypt right after his election giving a speech about freedom. This led to unrest in the entire region ultimately seeing a revolution in the entire region with people thinking that demonstrating in a downtown square brings freedom. Unfortunately, this quest for freedom brought chaos in Libya and Syria and were it not for the Egypt military taking charge saving the country from its freedom seekers, Egypt would also have fallen into chaos.

By 2014, chaos reigned in Iraq, Syria, Libya with Afghanistan teetering on the brink of another political collapse. Tensions rose as Russia invaded and took the Crimea and invaded parts of the Ukraine where Russian separatists shot down a Malaysian passenger airliner with 300 passengers killed.

As of the time this book was written, President Obama declared war on ISIS. He tried to put into place a coalition of European and Arab states to fight this new terrorist regime which had over ran parts of Syria and Iraq. ISIS was able to accomplish this including taking control of territory by stealing billions of military equipment the U.S. left behind for the Iraqi army to defend itself with. But, he violated the most basic principle of warfare as explained by Gen. Douglas MacArthur.

"Never start a war without having a plan of winning it and the resources to win".Obama's plan lack the most fundamental component of warfare "boots on the ground" and compounded his mistake by telling the terrorists that the U.S will just send airplanes and never any ground forces to finish the job. Even after the air strikes might have pulverized the ISIS, somebody has to go in on ground to "mop up" and restore order. That takes the combined effort of all coalition forces including the U.S. even if the U.S. might be a very small component. This mistaken decision is politically driven more than sound military strategy.

On the home front, Congress and the White House continued in deadlock. They were near paralysis on the budget and resolving chaos on immigration policy as more undocumented people continued crossing the borders. That placed horrendous economic and security concerns especially on the border states of Texas, Arizona and New Mexico.

In the summer of 2014, a near state of revolution unfolded in the small St. Louis suburban town of Ferguson when a white police officer shot and killed a black street vagrant. This resulted in riots and rising tensions again between blacks and whites at the refrain of "justice for all". There were cries about excessive police brutality and police starting to look like a military force with armored cars, tanks and SWAT wagons patrolling America's streets.

While all these things were unfolding, school killings with guns smuggled into schools by teenagers continued resulting even in a few massacres. Cries about better gun controls continued falling on deaf ears in Congress which was paralyzed by the National Rifle Association focused on selling more guns citing everyone's constitutional right.

Locally, elections became a joke as the Supreme Court allowed unlimited campaign contributions to candidates for office just about destroying the very essence of the democratic process.

Gunther Karger

The Miami Dade County commissioner election of August 2014 well illustrated how the local political process had become corrupted. Out of a district population of about 250,000, an unknown figure toppled the incumbent with only about 17,000 people voting and the incumbent lost by 688 votes. How? By the unions funding an unrelenting campaign using nearly $800,000 in campaign contributions basically paying $1,100 per winning vote. That's electing a person with only about 3% of the people voting for the winner. Is that democracy? No wonder more and more people simply gave up and no longer bothered to vote.

That was the state of sad affairs the U.S. and world faced as this book went to "press".

My legacy

There you have it. I bared my life to you in this book because that's all I have to leave behind. While I might have been able to contribute something while I breathed and walked this planet, unfortunately Shirley & I did not leave grand children to carry on the legacy of the Karger family into future generations. Nor did we leave the billions or even millions. However, continuing the tenor of my life, that being to do my best with whatever I do have each day, I am blessed to see another day, at age 81.

What would such best be? It is this book telling you and future generations who Gunther Karger was, where he came from and what he did during his 81 years. It is my strong belief that the experience of each person on this earth is unique. Whether a peasant carving out the basics of life or world renowned person, such person leaves something even though the peasant might just leave a microscopic grain on sands of time or a dynasty to be remembered for all times such as the pharos of ancient Egypt.

If I lived in a far future generation and was preparing to leave it behind as I now am, my legacy or as some might put it "My obituary" might be in the form of a hologram set into the fabric of that era's archives. Then, anyone for all time left in this universe, the story of Gunther could be visually seen and orally heard by going to a subject, time or name index. I would appear before you and tell it to you instead of you reading about it in a book. If this sounds like science fiction, remember that the science fiction of yesterday has become fact today and since I am a futurist, what I tell today as science fiction likely will become reality tomorrow.

Gunther Karger

Lets not now fail to mention Shirley because without question, she became part of my life early on and without her presence and partnership, my life would have been dramatically different. I would say that the force which created and still oversees the universe brought Shirley & I together, kept us together and guided us through our path of life together.

Now, to my final chapter, which tells about what kind of world and society this planet called Earth likely will become by the next generation which I will put as 20 years ahead. That sets time to the year 2035 and I most likely except for this book would have passed into the fabric of history. So, this becomes my legacy.

I should say that my foretelling of the near future is based on the assumption that the present political flavor of leadership continues until the 2020 election. If however, the politicians come to their senses immediately, start learning historical lessons and above all, shift their focus from their special interests to the best interest of the country, my foretelling would be somewhat different.

Welcome to the year 2035

Were I alive today at age 102, this is the world I would find myself in. How did we get here? What did the world have to experience to lead to such profound changes? What was the resource the world as a whole had to enable it to survive the near global collapse of the first 15 years of this century which I touched on in earlier chapters?

It is the inherent survival instinct in each of us and collectively as a society to find a way forward. To make us a better life as individuals and as a society. Perhaps this instinct was given us by the force that created the universe and still guides what's therein. (Earlier chapter on "Gunther's views on religion"). Maybe it's our basic driver that tells us we had enough and we don't want to take it anymore. It could be an event that brought everyone together in desperate search of a way to collectively survive. Maybe a strong real leader finally emerged capable to bring the fractious world together.

History tells how this happened. Here in this book, let's just accept that whatever it was and maybe it was a combination of all these factors, the world survived and here you are. I cannot say "here we are" because I no longer will be with you except in memory of a few and via this book. The important thing though is that the world did survive and it today is the year 2035.

Why did I pick this particular year? Because it's 20 years forward from the year this book was completed and I estimated that it would take about 20 years to transform our global society into what it could become. Twenty years also is a generation. Keep in mind that since the beginning of time, change accelerates and that acceleration increases exponentially with time. This means that future changes will be compressed into a shorter time. Consider just in my own lifetime how the world changed. My own eyes saw and my ears heard Adolph Hitler speak in downtown Berlin in 1939.

I witnessed the birth of the atomic age, participated and saw the revolution in communications and saw how this changed the way we live. Just over the past ten years, the world changed from a wired to a rapidly becoming wireless world.

Five years ago, if you went to work, you struggled in heavy traffic wasting hours on the road getting to work. Today, you are at work before even getting up by switching on your tablet computer by your bedside or go to the nearest coffee shop and sign in to work on your notebook. Where was same sex marriage five years ago? What about the rapidly evolving paperless medical office? Five years ago, Internet shopping was just starting and look where it is today? So don't be surprised to see transformational changes by the time the next 20 years roll by.

Making this futuristic prediction possible, I am using the tools I identified in the chapter "**Psychohistoric Morphology**" drawing from Dr. Isaac Asimov's science he calls "Psychohistory" set in his science fiction world and Dr. Robert Allen's "Morphological Creativity" conceived to solve the problems of the Cold War of the 60's.

So now, let's go to that timeport door and step through to the year 2035 to see what might be seen on the road getting there.

Changing Political System
2015-25

By the end of 2014, the people of the United States had tired of the increasing bickering between the political parties. The far right focused excessively on morality issues based on their brand of religion while the far left wanted to give whatever the havenots wanted regardless whether the country's <u>treasury</u> could afford it. At times, it seemed more important to define when life begins whether at birth or at conception than dealing with national security, resolving budget impasses in the congress and gun control while massacres continued at schools and public places.

People were tiring of the constant foreign policy blunders drawing the country into one war after another. Finally, when less and less people bothered to vote out of disgust for the poor quality of political candidates, so few people bothered to vote that no longer there appeared a democracy. Basically, the country became ruled by minority groups with elections decided not by how good the candidate was, but by how much money the candidate could amass to wage an effective advertising campaign.

As domestic violence continued rising along with falling confidence of politicians to even lower levels, small militias were organized throughout the country. These militias gradually grew joined by military veterans to a point at which they became a significant force. By 2018, so many people became disgusted with the political parties and democratic processes declining to near non existent levels that they actively sought to change the way the U.S. government functions. This led to the creation of the "People's Party" which allied itself with the growing militias.

By 2020, a small cadre of high ranking military officers including some generals had joined the People's Party and ran the their own candidate for President and sponsored many to run for Congress, state and local elections.

Their leader and presidential candidate was a three star general who had secretly worked with the "National Militia Council" (NMC) formulating a plan to restructure the way the United States would be run with a tilt toward a militarized rule.

The presidential candidate resigned from the Air Force to legally run for president. His campaign was focused on "Recover America for the people and once again return the country to world leadership". He won by a landslide heralding a new day and a new era for the United States. Not only did the general win by a wide margin, the People's Party"(PP) won majority in both Senate and House so therefore, PP secured control of the government. In a few months after the election, the people's Party had basically taken control over the Washington establishment and many state and local offices.

The first action taken by the new president was to call for a constitutional convention to bring the constitution up to date as it no longer fit the new times. After all, it was written nearly 250 years before and, although its fundamental principles remained, some adjustments were badly needed.

One such change dealt with the qualifications of the President. We had evolved to a far more complex world driven technology, globalization and the absolute necessity for countries to cooperate rather than remain isolationist.

A person leading a country therefore needs to have some experience leading. Unfortunately, since the constitution only requires to be a natural born citizen at least 35 years old, under this rule, a Downs syndrome afflicted person could qualify . The revised constitutional qualification requirements included executive experience in managing something and minimum educational achievements including specifically extensive knowledge of world history and the evolution of military strategy. Just having a law degree became no longer enough. Presidential candidates would have to appear before a "Presidential Qualification Council" . No longer would it be possible for a candidate to run for president solely because of excellence in making speeches.

The second significant change was to adopt the parliamentary system similar to that of the UK. Specifically, if the president loses the confidence of the congress or by the people as a whole, new elections would become required. This change was deemed necessary to prevent the governmental paralysis that occurred during the 2005 – 2015 period which at one time even led to the shutdown of the government.

The third major constitutional change was the addition of responsibility by citizens to vote to regain a level of democratic process that had been lost. The change was the addition of a new requirement applicable to residents of all states. If a person does not vote in two consecutive elections, that person loses all financial benefits associated with property taxes on personal residences, such as Homestead Exemption. The purpose of this is to make it costly not to exercise the privilege of voting for citizens.

The fourth change addressed the problem of public assistance and welfare recipients increasing in numbers to the point of having a major influence on elections. This became a significant problem during Obama's regime when excessive liberals and social service minded people ran for office in local elections and too many people became dependent on such elected officials leading to budget problems for local municipalities as well as the federal government. To resolve this dilemma, the right to vote became suspended for anyone living on public assistance including unemployment and direct welfare payments for more than six months.

The fifth change required political candidates to approve campaign materials including flyers, telephone calls and radio/TV ads paid for by political action groups. It therefore would no longer be possible for a candidate to disavow knowledge of an ad that says the opponent poisons children unless that allegation is supported by evidence. This would make a stab at squeezing gross lies out of campaigns which would be sufficiently effective for the accused candidate to lose the election

The sixth change was the declaration that English is the official language and the ballots must be only in English. The basis for this requirement is not to exclude voters but to ensure that all who vote understand better what they are voting for. Mainstream media such as TV and newsprint is in English and if the voter can't read or understand main stream communications, they shouldn't vote.

The seventh significant change was the creation of a constitutionally mandated National Emergency Council(NEC) to consist of the President, Speaker of the House, Senate Majority Leader, Secretary of Defense, Director of National Intelligence, Secretary of State, Chief Justice of Supreme Court and Attorney General. The NEC would have the authority to declare a national emergency and take such actions as it deems required to preserve national security.

One specific authority the NEC would have is to activate and immediately deploy the Rapid Reaction Unit(RRU) to protect the security of United States. The RRU was assigned to the Military department responsible for the Combined Services Special Forces but also under the direction of the NEC should an emergency immediate reaction deployment arise. This RRU would be authorized to call up whatever resources as may be required to deploy military capability to anywhere on earth on orders from the NEC. Among resources available to the NEC will the X51A hypersonic UAV capable of delivering a significant bomb to anywhere on the globe within 2 hours and the targeting of satellite based laser weapons. The RRU reached full operational capability by the year 2025.

The eight amendment would be to change the terms for the House of Representatives to increase from two to four years. The two year term is too short because too much of it is spent raising money and campaigning for re-election and too little to actual work addressing the needs of the country.

Globalization of World Security

While changes rapidly evolved in the United States during the post 2015 period, so did they also globally. The conflict between sectarian based nationalism and the relentlessly spreading globalization of commerce driven by accelerating technology advances reached intolerable levels by 2016.

President Obama with the help of Secretary of State John Kerry and UK Prime Minister Cameron had succeeded to form a coalition of nations including Saudi Arabia and Egypt which by the spring of 2015 had seriously degraded ISIS but it still had pockets of significant strength as were remnants of Al Quaeda and others in Somalia, Pakistan, Indonesia and the West Africa area including Libya.

The major countries including Russia, European Union, UK, China, Japan, Saudi Arabia finally realized that sectarian based military conflicts had reached massively destructive levels and had to be reigned in. Their economies were being increasingly impacted. They gradually started to realize that it was better to capitulate to the relentless globalization movement than constantly dealing with terrorism and realized that embracing peaceful globalization was far preferable. They finally began to realize that nationalism could be preserved and even be enhanced if the nations worked together to prevent sectarian based terrorism. They realized that they no longer could afford the high cost of military conflict and moreover, recognized that advanced technology destructive military capability in the wrong hands could devastate their countries.

The new U.S. president elected in 2020 initiated contact with heads of state of all major countries and Israel to establish a standing international anti terrorist rapid response unit.

Near the end of his first term in 2023, he had obtained agreement with funding commitments from Russia, UK. Germany, France, India, China, Saudi Arabia, Egypt, Israel, Canada and Mexico.

By 2025 and into his second presidential term, the international response team became operational. With international terrorism rapidly declining, it assumed the historic role of the United Nations Security Council which became disbanded due to its increasing irrelevance.

The decline in terrorism had a positive impact on national budgets allowing the released economic stimulus to some degree replace military spending. This provided a huge economic benefit which in the Mideast helped replace terrorism with income producing jobs which in and of itself accelerated the decline of violence and terrorism. The world was rapidly learning that hunger drives terrorism while full stomachs reduces it.

Global initiatives in space

Early in the president's second term, he led the United States into an initiative to create an international space exploration consortium where specifically multiple nations would cooperatively in single projects and restarted a major international consortium sponsored manned space program.

The world had finally learned that it's better for domestic economies to cooperate than fight one another, Russia, Japan, China, Germany, UK, Australia and France jumped easily aboard this project. Cape Canaveral and the Baikonour Cosmodrome in Kazakstan became the two major space ports while the HQ for the international space consortium became established at the Houston space Center.

By 2035, the international consortium was fully operational even with an outpost on the moon and was planning for a Mars manned mission. By 2035, this consortium already intercepted and destroyed three major asteroids in space as one of the missions became Earth defense against space borne threats.

The second president elected under the revised constitution continued the initiatives of the first. He established a global financial and investment fraud commission recognizing that financial operations had become so globally connected that a single regulatory and anti fraud system was needed.

By 2035, the world as defined by earth standards had become far more peaceful than ever before, terrorism had nearly been erased and hunger was a rarity even among the least developed areas.

Criminals and terrorists had learned that the effectiveness of the global antiterrorism unit which had been expanded to major crime control and a force which could rarely be avoided. This fear of apprehension and very serious consequences had dramatically reduced major crime and global financial fraud.

The United Nations had by 2035 become restructured to focus on health and environmental issues and through this, had made major strides reducing epidemics and poor health habits in the remaining under developed regions.

Globalization had by 2035 reached a major milestone as the United Nations secured an agreement from all nations to issue a global passport and established a global system of issuing visas along with international migration standards. This once and for all resolved the illegal immigration crisis the United States experienced in the first 15 years of the century.

Late in 2035, the big news was that the Atacama Radio Astronomical Observatory high on the Atacama, Chile desert had detected signals from deep space indicating an intelligence was trying to communicate with Earth. This focused Earth into even greater cooperation among nations as the International Space Defense organization was formed to face this new challenge, this time from outer space.

Thus, I conclude my book and my legacy. I hope I have brought new perspective and in particular, a higher level of hope for a great future.

With this, I bid you farewell!

"It's not the years in your life that count.
It is the life in your years that matter."
Abraham Lincoln

Appendix
Special Recognition

As I transitioned through life, I was fortunate to be given significant recognition for my pioneering work in space and missiles, national security and community service. I included a few of these mementos with a commentary about what they represent.

Gunther Karger

United States

Securities and Exchange Commission

Certificate of Appreciation

Presented to

Gunther Karger

IN RECOGNITION OF HIS TIRELESS EFFORTS ON BEHALF OF THE
INVESTOR COMMUNITY AND HIS GENEROSITY IN DEVOTING UNCOUNTED
HOURS TO STUDYING KEY ISSUES BEFORE THE SEC, AND PROVIDING THE
COMMISSION WITH TIMELY , CONCISE AND PERSUASIVE ANALYSIS.

BY HELPING TO KEEP THE COMMISSION FOCUSED ON THE NEEDS
AND CONCERNS OF RETAIL INVESTORS, GUNTHER HELPED MAKE
AMERICA'S FINANCIAL MARKETS MORE EQUITABLE AND FAIR FOR ALL.

December 14, 2012

Mary. L. Schapiro

Mary L. Schapiro, Chairman

**This special recognition was presented to me
personally by Chairman Mary L. Shapiro, during her final
days as Chairman of the Securities and Exchange
Commission(SEC) when she also personally declared me
"Honorary U.S. Federal Special Agent" and placed on my
head the " Enforcement Agent" cap.**

Presented to me by S.W. Herwall, President of the IEEE International in recognition of serving as Chairman of the Cape Canaveral Section with 3000 members during the Moon program

THE **INSTITUTE OF ELECTRICAL AND ELECTRONICS ENGINEERS, INC.**

takes pleasure in presenting this Certificate to

Gunther Karger

in recognition and appreciation of his valued services and contributions as

Chairman
Canaveral Section

1968

S. W. Herwall
President

Gunther Karger

Proclamation

WHEREAS: *Gunther Karger was born on March 16, 1933 in Schmieheim, Germany; and*

WHEREAS: *Gunther at age six, escaped Nazi Germany in 1939 when his parents sent him away on a transport of children to Sweden where he lived for seven years. He carried a single suitcase containing a few pictures of his parents and Schmieheim family and the only picture of his friend, Hanna Baumann, in existence; and*

WHEREAS: *Gunther's family were victims of the Gurs concentration camp in France, leaving Gunther the sole survivor of the Offenheimers, his grandparents' name; and*

WHEREAS: *In 1951, Gunther Karger graduated high school in New Jersey as valedictorian and joined the United States Air Force, working as a research engineer in aerospace sciences; and*

WHEREAS: *Gunther Karger and his wife, Shirley, married in 1953, have two sons, and reside in Homestead, Florida; and*

WHEREAS: *Gunther was named "Outstanding Young Man of America" in 1967 for his contributions to the space program and national security; and*

WHEREAS: *Gunther authored Thieves on Wall Street: Survival Guide for the Investor and Wall Street and Government Fraud in an effort to bring the individual investor an ounce of truth and straight talk amidst the pounds of misleading spin from Wall Street; and*

WHEREAS: *On December 14, 2012, the United States Securities and Exchange Commission recognized Gunther's tireless efforts on behalf of the investor community and his generosity in devoting uncounted hours to studying key issues and providing the Commission with timely, concise and persuasive analysis. By helping to keep the commission focused on the needs and concerns of retail investors, Gunther helped make America's financial markets more equitable and fair for all; and*

WHEREAS: *Gunther Kruger is an inspirational and extraordinary man, corporate manager, leader in technology, author, lecturer and columnist, recently turning 80 years young after overcoming all obstacles as he survived the holocaust and the transition from one foster home to another.*

NOW, THEREFORE, I, Steven C. Bateman, *the Mayor of the City of Homestead, Florida, do hereby proclaim this 17th day of April, 2013 as*

Gunther Karger Day

In Homestead.

IN WITNESS WHEREOF, *I hereunto set my hand and cause the Great Seal of the City of Homestead, to be affixed.*

Mayor Steven C. Bateman

City of Homestead

Patricia Fairclough, Councilwoman	Steven C. Bateman, Mayor	Judy Waldman, Councilwoman
Elvis R. Maldonado, Councilman	Jon Burgess, Vice-Mayor	Stephen R. Shelley, Councilman
	Jimmie L. Williams, III, Councilman	

This was presented April 17, 2013 to me at the Homestead City Council meeting in recognition my contributions as part of recognizing National Holocaust Remembrance week.

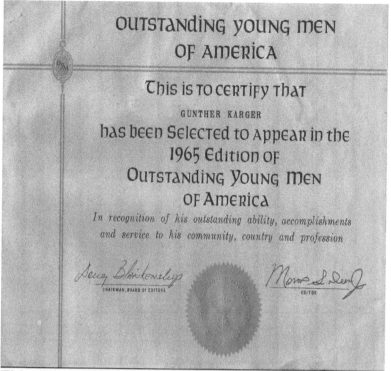

This was awarded me for my contribution to the Space Program as a scientist and developing a national security system designed to help the country react and recover after a nuclear enemy attack destroying most American major cities and military bases. I had been assigned to serve as Project Manager of Strategic Command Control system in a post nuclear attack situation. This was presented to me by Junior Chamber of Commerce International while we lived at Cape Canaveral, then America's primary space port.

Gunther named "Missile and Space Pioneer" by Cape Canaveral Rocket Society

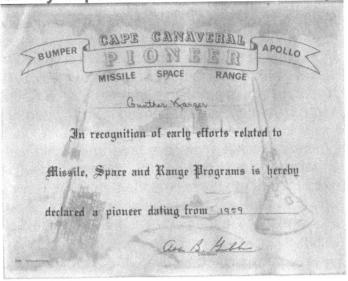

I was one of three engineers credited with the design of Courier Satellite, the first active communications satellite launched 1960 from Cape Canaveral, while I worked at ITT Labs in New Jersey. When we moved to the Cape Canaveral area in 1964, I became involved with the leadership of the electrical engineers who developed communications that supported launches of missiles and space vehicles including the Apollo moon program and deep space probes. I personally worked with Dr. Vernher von Braun whose rocket team originally from Peenemunde, Germany had developed the V-2 rocket which was the world's first liquid fueled long range rocket based on the original design by Dr. Robert Goddard who is considered the "Father of rocketry".

Von Braun expanded the V-2 design into "Bumper alter becoming "Redstone" which became the backbone of America's rocket program through Apollo. As a historical note, there, were significant differences between the German V-1 and V-2 rockets.

The V-1 was the original "Flying Bomb" used to nearly destroy London. It was a shorter range what we today might called "Unmanned turbo jet powered bomb with wings", the V-2 was a longer range liquid fueled rocket which became the backbone of the U.S. strategic missile program and basis for the Redstone and Apollo rockets all stemming from Dr. Vernher von Braun's earlier work. The German influence on America's rocket and space program should never be underestimated. That the U.S. first reached von Braun's rocket team from Peenemunde before the Russians who also were after them became a critical factor in U.S. prevailing in the cold War instead of the Soviet Union.

Clifford Mattox, one of the original U.S. intelligence officers who retrieved von Braun and his German rocket team from Germany after WW II ended became our good friend. He invited me to the inner circle of the Cape Canaveral Rocket Pioneers which officially designated me "Missile, Space and Range Pioneer.

Referring to my dream, as a ten year old refugee in Sweden having fled the ravages of the Holocaust, reading science fiction comics about Flash Gordon and Buck Rogers, this fulfilled that dream.

Gunther Karger

The following certificate was awarded for my
participation in the first test flight for the Saturn V, the
launch vehicle which was ultimately used by the U.S.
Apollo ...

The Boeing Company
Boeing Atlantic Test Center

Certificate Of Award

PRESENTED TO

Gunther Karger

IN RECOGNITION OF YOUR PERSONAL CONTRIBUTION TO THE TEAM EFFORT
WHICH CULMINATED IN THE HIGHLY SUCCESSFUL FLIGHT OF THE FIRST
AS-501 APOLLO/SATURN VEHICLE ON 9 NOVEMBER 1967.

YOUR SIGNIFICANT CONTRIBUTION GREATLY ASSISTED THE SATURN V
PROGRAM AND WAS VITAL TO THE OVERALL APOLLO 4 MISSION
ACCOMPLISHMENT.

J./J. Cully
KSC SATURN V MANAGER

A./M. Johnston
BATC DIRECTOR

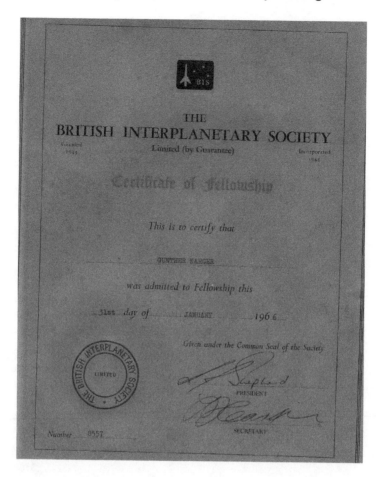

The British Interplanetary Society awarded me in 1966
the status of "Fellow". This society was founded in
1933, the year of my birth, to promote the exploration of
space and astronomy. This Society recognized me for
my contributions to Space Exploration the year I served
as Chairman of the Canaveral Section of the Institute of
Electrical and Electronics Engineers(IEEE).
I consider this a miraculous achievement for that six
year old boy sitting on that black suitcase in the
Swedish train station having just fled for his life from
certain death in Germany if his parents had not shipped
him out of the country.

Arbitrator 2006

Member, NASD Dispute Resolution
Board of Arbitrators

Gunther Karger

Phillip M. Aidikoff
Chair-National Arbitration
and Mediation Committee

George H. Friedman
Executive Vice President
NASD Dispute Resolution
Director, Arbitration Program

Date: May 18, 2006
Arbitrator Number: A34200

Resulting from my experience in the financial service industry as publisher, broker, investment adviser and author, I had been invited to become Arbitrator for the NASD (National Association of Securities Dealers) which later became FINRA (Financial Industry Regulatory Authority serving the New York Stock Exchange, NASDAQ and all major stock exchanges.)

Before being "Certified" and allowed to serve as 'Arbitrator", I was required to complete extensive training and pass a comprehensive examination consisting of applicable law and regulations. The attendees at the training sessions were primarily retired judges, lawyers and senior industry professionals.

As "Arbitrator", I was given judicial powers similar to a judge to hear cases, call witnesses, and make final rulings on cases that came before the Arbitration Panel.